MW00464810

BACK FROM THE
SHADOW
OF DEATH

FULFILLING LIFE'S MISSION WITH GOD'S HELP

WRITTEN BY

MARWIN STRONG

PUBLISHED BY FIDELI PUBLISHING, INC.

Back from the Shadow of Death
Copyright © 2020, Marwin Strong

ISBN: 978-1-948638-13-5

Transcription, additional interviews and editing by
A. K. Bell, author and editor, Muncie, Indiana

Cover, About the Author and About the Editor
photos by Amy Payne, aimedphotography.com.

Author Marwin Strong is an international spiritual
leader and speaker, Dallas, Texas.
Contact the author @:
marwinstrong30@gmail.com

Published by Fideli Publishing, Inc.
119 West Morgan Street
Martinsville, IN 46151
www.FideliPublishing.com

This book is dedicated to the memory of
my mother Martha Strong
who passed away
February 3, 2019.

Rest in Heaven, Momma.

ACKNOWLEDGEMENTS

Family, friends, educators, coaches and mentors helped me in my journey including the creation of this book. This work is based on a 2017 interview at my alma mater Ball State University. Journalism student at the time, Charity Monroe, interviewed me as part of the African American Alumni Project. Catch it on YouTube: (https://www.youtube.com/watch?v=QWu_ishnn-A&-feature=youtube (uploaded March 29, 2019).

Considering where I came from, I never would have dreamt it would be possible for me to finish college. I earned my degrees in Muncie, Indiana including my associates from Ivy Tech Community College and my bachelors from Ball State University. I taught students at both schools on how to be successful in college and in life. I thank both institutions for these opportunities.

I thank my colleague, mentor and friend Ball State University professor and counselor Nancy Harper for giving me my first chance at college-level teaching. She has supported me throughout my professional career. Nancy pushed me to continue my mission of reaching out to troubled youth, and I wouldn't be where I am without her help.

I'd like to give a special thank you also to Jan Carter-Goldman, my hospital mom. She gave me strength and inspiration when I needed it most and continues to be my friend today.

Coaches, you helped me believe in myself. That includes Mr. Wilson at Washington Carver Elementary, Coach Francis Lafferty of Northside Middle School and Coach Charlie Titus from the University of Massachusetts in Boston. I thank you.

I thank my long-time friend and editor Allison K. Bell for our collaboration on this important project. You're a woman of your word. I look forward to our next one.

Without the extended Strong family in the City of Muncie, I would not be alive today. Many of you helped save me, most importantly my momma, Martha Strong. We love and miss you. I thank my father, Michael Hall, who showed me you can change your life and be a blessing.

I love my brothers and sisters Sylvia West, Melinda Strong, Stevie Strong, Georgia Strong, Michael Strong, Michelle Davis and Danielle Davis. On my dad's side, I thank my brothers: Tony Baines, Tyrone Heard and Michael Heard; and my sisters Tonya and Tawanda Heard and Brittany Claybrook.

My very special grandmothers, Josephine Strong and Rosemary Long, helped raise me. Thank you also to my many aunties, uncles and cousins in the extended Strong family. It took a village to raise me and then some!

I thank my good friends, former NBA star Bonzi Wells, Muncie lawyer John Brooke, Circuit Court Judge Marianne Vorhees and former Ball State University President Jo Ann Gora. President Gora was Chancellor when I was at University of Massachusetts) and I was grateful to continue our friendship when she arrived to be BSU's President in Muncie.

My churches have been a source of new life, hope and community including Greater New Life Worship Center in Indianapolis, Indiana, and The Potter's House in Dallas, Texas. My identity also comes from being part of the Muncie community.

Everyday people, who have come together from all walks of life, and from hundreds of churches and organizations have supported my anti-drug and violence efforts throughout the years. Numerous community leaders and friends have offered leadership in Muncie in these efforts. It's impossible to thank them individually. Please know how deeply I appreciate you, and I know your work is critical.

Thanks to the leadership at Texas Can Academy in Dallas, Texas, I am continuing my mission across the country. The amazing students there continue to inspire me every day. Thank you to the leadership and students at the academy for the opportunity to teach and coach this regional powerhouse team.

Last, but not least, I love and thank my children Dalvin, Malea, Zion, and Samara Strong, and Daizya Rankin. You are all my life. I'm so proud of your accomplishments and how you keep on bettering yourselves.

Finally, I thank God. You loved me, and you saved me, so I could have a life and do good in others' lives.

Lord, I will not let you down!

—Marwin Strong

FORWARD

When I first met **Marwin Strong** in 2004, he was a tall, lanky 27-year-old who had just become the first African American housing manager at the inner-city Parkview Apartments in Muncie, Indiana. At the time, I was the managing director of a United Way community development initiative called Partners for Community Impact. Marwin's reputation as a game changer in the community preceded him, and I needed his help.

Marwin and I grew up in different worlds, but we connected quickly. We shared a passion to make the community safer and to help families succeed. Marwin shared his story with me of how he barely escaped the drugs and violence in his high-poverty neighborhood growing up in Muncie. I shared with Marwin how I had spent several years of my childhood overseas, often witnessing the fallout from the violence of war.

My newscaster father, Steve Bell, covered the Vietnam War for ABC Radio and Television in the late 1960s and early 70s. We lived primarily in Hong Kong because Dad didn't think it was safe for us to live full-time in Vietnam. But on regular trips to Saigon, the ravages of that war hit home. As children, my sister Hilary and I could hear shooting in the streets and the "chop, chop" of battle helicopters going to and from the war; we witnessed wounded soldiers, often with no limbs, who were left with no choice but to beg on the streets; and we saw families with children who lived in such poverty they had nothing but huts made of tarps to protect them, even from the monsoon rains.

At six years old, I was keenly aware that my father's life was frequently in danger. Despite his years covering the front lines, miraculously, Dad lived through that period. In fact, both of my parents lived into their 80s. Dad made a career transition to teaching in 1992 as the first Edward and Virginia Ball Endowed Chair in Telecommunications at Ball State University in Muncie.

My children and I followed my parents to Muncie in 1998, and my sister Hilary lived just a few hours away in Michigan, so we were all close the last 20 years of their lives. I'm grateful we had so much time with them before they died. I'm also grateful they instilled in all of us the conviction that we should never take our good lives for granted, and that we have a responsibility to help others as much as possible.

Working with Marwin Strong and others on the Weed & Seed project in Muncie had a tremendous impact on my life. I'm grateful for the good work of all my colleagues and collaborators in that effort and appreciate your continuing accomplishments. I'm honored to have the opportunity to write this book and continue our work together.

Our families have celebrated joyful times. As an ordained church elder, Marwin has sealed tightly nearly 150 marriages. In 2013, one of those happy weddings was mine. Marwin and I have also mourned together. He has performed way too many funerals, many for his own childhood friends or their family members. We have even lost children who were friends with our own kids in school who died from drug-related shootings or overdoses.

Our families have also mourned together recently over the natural deaths of loved ones. Both my parents died in 2019 only eight months apart. Marwin also lost his beloved momma, Martha Strong, last year. The hole left by the loss of these three has been so great that moving forward has been challenging for both of us.

Fulfilling the commitment that I made to Marwin 14 years ago, to help him write this book, has been healing. What an honor it is for me to help bring Marwin's story to light. It fulfills a mission we share. Rising together has helped us heal a lot faster than standing apart.

Some voices MUST be heard. Marwin Strong's is one of them.

— A. K. Bell, editor

INTRODUCTION

I committed my first robbery at the age of nine because I was hungry. I became a drug dealer to feed my family. It's by the Grace of God that I did not become a statistic.

Many black men in the United States don't live past the age of 22 (Bond. 2016). That meant my chances of getting out of poverty and drugs wasn't that great. I didn't come from a faith-based home. I went to church on Easter, but I didn't care too much about God.

At the lowest time in my life, God seized on me and made me change. I am a man who walks in two worlds, a man who has seen two different ways of life. That's why sometimes people say I talk funny. I speak proper English, but sometimes Ebonics comes out. That's me, man! So, that's how I'm going to tell my story. I'm writin' about my experience in Christian context. But this is for everyone.

I don't cuss now. But you gonna hear some in this book because I got to be real with you to tell this story. I don't believe in cussing. But back in the drug world, that was my life. I'm a hundred percent real, so I'm gonna tell my story for real. A lot of people don't embrace realness. I don't want to have people wonder who I am. So, I'm going to tell it like it is.

It's the TRUTH.

If I can change, anybody can. My wish is for everybody to know, even though you weren't born with the best, you can be the best. That's my mission, to tell you that. I'm gonna do it with His help.

To God be the Glory.

Psalm 23

¹The Lᴏʀᴅ is my shepherd; I shall not want.

²He maketh me to lie down in green pastures: he leadeth me beside the still waters.

³He restoreth my soul: he leadeth me in the paths of righteousness for his name's sake.

⁴Yea, though I walk through the valley of the shadow of death, I will fear no evil: for thou art with me; thy rod and thy staff they comfort me.

⁵Thou preparest a table before me in the presence of mine enemies: thou anointest my head with oil; my cup runneth over.

⁶Surely goodness and mercy shall follow me all the days of my life: and I will dwell in the house of the Lᴏʀᴅ forever.

King James Version (KJV)

BACK FROM THE
SHADOW
OF DEATH
FULFILLING LIFE'S MISSION WITH GOD'S HELP

TABLE OF CONTENTS

PART I
SHADOW OF DEATH

PART II
INTO THE LIGHT

PART I
SHADOW OF DEATH

Eleven-year-old Marwin with friends at a cabin in Heekin Park, Muncie, Indiana.

Marwin, at 18 years old, often wore his favorite jacket from a popular black clothing designer, Fubu.

CHAPTER 1

LIVING A LIFE OF WANT

"I lived a life of hopelessness"

My family was hustlers, and thieves and people who went to prison. People who killed people. We was the black sheep of the family, and demons was all around me.

I didn't come from a faith-based home. I was raised in an environment where religion was not a big issue. I didn't care nothing about that. I didn't know Him, and I didn't care about Him. I either lived, or I died. That's how it was cause God wasn't my source. I lived a life of hopelessness. I didn't care nothing about God. All I cared about was me.

I was born in a very, low poverty area in Muncie, Indiana, on January 2, 1977 (City-Data.com. 2020).

All my childhood I just wanted to be first. I thought, "Momma, you couldn't have gone and given birth to me the day before that? I wanted to be a New Year's baby."

Now I loved my momma, but I always thought that I just wasn't convenient for her. Momma told me she was all dolled up that night I was supposed to be born. She was ready to go to a party. She was still pretty in them heels, even though she was hanging out big since she was pregnant. When her water broke at that party, she just kept right on dancing. She didn't want to miss the fun. I was second. She waited until the next day, the second of January, to have me.

Even though we didn't live the church life, my Momma didn't mess around. We always said, "Yes, Ma'am." I learned quick she did not want to ask me twice to do something. If my momma heard me cuss when I was a young man, boy, she'd have slapped me in the head with the telephone. I'm not talking about no wimpy-assed smart phone, but those big old gray, hammer-like rocks. Child protective services didn't care back then. Shit, that hurt.

Even though Momma was strict, she and I was close. But I didn't always know which one of us was the parent. Even at a young age, I was my momma's protector. She used to date different guys. These guys sold drugs, and they was doing drugs. She'd get in fist fights with them. I was just a kid, but I tried to get between my mom and the other guys. I watched a guy break my momma's face. I was with my momma when she had a nervous breakdown. Sometimes we both just sat down and cried. I would tell her everything would be alright. I loved my momma, so it really hurt me to see her hurt.

Sometimes we didn't see Momma for days. She had a job, sometimes two or three. We didn't know what kind of jobs. That meant we kids was at home alone a lot. Child Protective Services would come. We would turn off the lights and hide in the closets. We'd look out for 'em. They'd show up, and off we would go to our designated spots. Considering all we went through; it was by the grace of God that we wasn't separated by child services.

Sometimes when Momma wasn't there, I called up my Grandma Josephine. She'd walk for miles to take care of us. No matter how far away she lived, she'd be there to take care of her grandbabies. We'd live at Grandma's sometimes when Momma was out working. The tidy apartment was kind of empty, but it had lots of family pictures and vanilla colored walls like most people.

I could always smell the beans and cabbage on Grandma's stove. All us kids piled onto a big mattress shoved inside a closet to sleep. Inside that house, we felt safe even if we heard gunshots outside. We got so used to them, we just slept right through it.

I didn't really know that I was poor 'til I got older. Sometimes we didn't even have the basics. We just thought everybody lived like that: house full of roaches and mice; lights being cut off; water being cut off; gas and electric sometimes gone for weeks. When the water got cut off, we had to get some from my neighbor's home and boil it to get hot water for baths.

I didn't have the nicest clothes. I often wore my sister's old clothes and my brother's old socks. I'd get my sister's Jordache or Lee jeans and roll up the cuffs so I wouldn't trip on them. We all had to trade clothing items before school to find enough pieces to get out the door.

After school, we ran to the Multicultural Community Center. We called it the Multi. I took karate for no cost during the summers. Sometimes we would go there just to get free lunches. Some days that was the only meal we ate that day.

Like I said, I didn't have much church in my youth. Only reason I went was because I was hungry. Grace Baptist used to come by and pick us up in a white bus and take us to the church in the white community. When you got quiet, you got a hot dog, some potato chips and a dollar. You just can't say nothing at the service. That was the quietest I ever been.

Most people we knew ate fast food cause they thought it was cheap. But for us, we didn't have enough money for McDonald's. We sat outside across the street from the McDonald's on Madison Street for hours some days waiting until the store closed at night. Then we'd go diggin' for treasure. We'd take the food that the workers threw out in the trash and then go home and microwave them. We thought that was heaven. That's how we got our fast food.

When we could, we made a few dollars by turning in bottles for recycling. We'd walk for blocks to the sanitation department. We called to the workers, raised them bottles up and said, "Hey, you got 10 cents a bottle?" When we got money, me and my older brother Stevie, we'd go get candy bars and ice cream. That's what we lived on. We didn't know about healthy food. We just didn't know better.

When you in the hood, you don't get a Kroger or nothing. We kids would go to the Village Pantry, a gas station on the corner. It was expensive and had no healthy stuff to eat. It was hard to find fresh fruit. I understand the dynamics of living off pork and beans and hotdogs.

One summer day when I was nine, I was walking home with some friends from the local public pool. It was hot outside that summer. The ground was so hot I felt it through my ratty shoes. We passed by a convenience store on the way home called Ryan's, and all my friends went in there to get a cold coke. Everyone went in except one of my friends, Chad, and me. We was upset cause we ain't got no money. They was getting cold drinks, and we couldn't get nothin.'

So, Chad and I walked on ahead of them. A few blocks down we saw the ice cream man riding by. Chad had a butterfly knife. We robbed that ice cream man. We didn't want the money. We just wanted the ice cream. We grabbed that ice cream and ran, climbing out of sight up into a pear tree, and we ate that ice cream. But that relief was only temporary. When we came down, the police was waiting.

Chad tried to vouch for me. He had the knife, so he said he was the one that pulled it out. But since I was around him when he did it, the police still said I was guilty as charged. But Chad insisted it was him. He took some of the heat off me, my friend. I never forget him for that. He explained he had the knife and took the rap.

The cops, they was actually nice compared to what was comin.' They put us in the cop car to wait for our parents to get there. I had scarier things to think about, my momma. She came storming over. I think even the cops feared her. That might have made them have mercy on me. We wasn't charged. Chad pleaded with my mom not to whoop me too bad. "Please Mrs. Strong, it was all my idea. I had the knife. It wasn't Marwin's fault."

Chad tried. But he couldn't save me from Momma. She charged over to the police car and said, "When we go home…. I'm gonna tell you!" I knew what was comin.' Back then you could whoop kids with sticks and cords and phones. Momma had a great aim. She whooped me bad that time. She told me, "You're gonna be punished for this for a long time." That whooping left flesh wounds. For a while, I did seriously question my choices after that. I had a sense like, "Hey, you can't do that. That's the wrong way to go about it. Even though you're hungry, you gotta eat what you got."

My momma tried to whoop the demons out of me, but it was too late. I had already ate fruit from the wrong tree.

Samara Strong, Martha Strong and Dalvin Strong (2009).

Marwin at 17 years old.

Left to right: Marwin Strong, Michael Strong, Steven Strong, Sylvia West, Michelle Davis, Danielle Davis, Melinda Strong and Georgia Strong (2003).

CHAPTER 2

I DIDN'T SEE NO SHEPHERD

"...Oh, my siblings and me, we could fight!"

My house was all kids all the time. We was kind of three families in one. My dad had 10 kids altogether. With all my dad's kids, and all my mom's kids, we had 16 sisters and brothers total. There was eight of us, including me, living with my mom. My three older siblings had one daddy. Me and my two next siblings had my daddy. And the youngest two, the twins, they had another daddy. My daddy was a pimp and heroin addict, so you can imagine, my childhood wasn't a fine and dandy one.

Momma's family, the Strong family, had two sides. We was the black sheep of the family. People on the other side of the family would say, "Don't go around them." We was always under the microscope, and people just expected we was up to no good.

Sometimes you couldn't blame them for thinking that. Now I love all my siblings. My brothers and sisters was always tight knitted. But oh, my siblings and me, we could fight! We'd yell and scream about clothes, food, and tattle talin'. But my siblings and me raised each other.

It got especially hard when we kids realized my mother was sick. We figured out she had alcoholism. She had multiple breakdowns, especially when my little sisters came along, my twin sisters, Michelle and Danielle. It was hard on her because they was the babies, and they was spoiled brats. (Don't worry, my sisters, I love y'all now!) Those two would fight in a minute. Momma may have had that post-partum depression, too.

My oldest sister Sylvia was the breadwinner. She was the mother of us, and she had to grow up early. Sylvia would get us up for school and made sure we did what we had to do. Everybody had to listen to my sister Sylvia. We still do to this day. She's a social worker now.

My next sister, Melinda, was a cunning, sneaky type of person as a kid. She would always find trouble and get me right in it! She wanted to venture off into the world to see what life was about. She is now in the restaurant business.

My big brother Stevie was the one who I always looked up to and depended on. He was a wrestler, a big strong guy. What was funny was we called him, "Little Stevie." No one messes with Little Stevie. No one. Stevie protected me and made sure nobody messed with me. Even if I could fight on my own, he never let me. He had to protect his little brother. I'll tell you more about what happened to Stevie later.

As for me? I was the middle child. I was always braggin' that I was the favorite. I thought I was going to be the last one of Momma's kids, "the Baby." I would make all my other siblings so mad. They got mad every year we celebrated my birthday. I'd be celebrating with my sisters Georgia, Sylvia and Melinda, and my brother Stevie. Because it was so close to Christmas, I got all the presents. They couldn't believe it. Oooh, they was all mad.

After me was my sister, Georgia. When she was first born, I didn't want her to be around. I didn't want her to be born. Like I said, I thought I was going to be the last child. So, Georgia and I always feuded, but secretly I loved her to death. I made sure nobody could mess with her but me.

I would get so mad at her that one time I bit her finger. When that sent her screamin,' I thought that was funny. So, I'd get her again. I bit it so bad so many times, I put a little scar right there that lasted for the longest time. It's gone now. Momma, she tore my butt up when she found out about that.

Georgia, she was tough, man. I think that was thanks to me. She had always been outspoken. Nobody was wonderin' how she felt. But deep down her heart was so soft, so beautiful and so big. I don't think she wanted me to know. I guess she forgave me. I'm so proud of her. She's a pharmacy tech now.

Then I have another brother, Michael. We called him "Boo." I always protected him just like Little Stevie protected me. I raised Michael, and that was a job man. He would just wander off. You'd find him in the middle of the night climbing on cabinets, eating cranberry sauce or sweet corn. I was the one that had to tell him to get down. Little old me! He's a cook now. He musta learned somethin' from all those cranberries and sweet corn.

Then Momma had twins, my sisters Michelle and Danielle. They were the last kids for my mother. They was fighting all the time. Michelle, she works at Ball State University in Muncie now. And Danielle is at the Holiday Inn. Those are my babies.

From back left, counterclockwise: Marwin Strong, Michelle Davis, Georgia Strong, Martha Strong, Danielle Davis and Sylvia West (2018).

It was a full house all those years. It was a full house and no shepherd to be found. At least that was what I thought. I know now, I just wasn't listening.

Marwin at his church, New Life Worship Center in Indianapolis, after his conversion following his release from the hospital (2003).

CHAPTER 3

LOOKING FOR GREENER PASTURES

"Watch him jump!"

My momma and siblings and me, we moved around a lot. I would go to one elementary school and then another. We had to move every time Momma couldn't get enough money to pay the rent. Finally, when I was about 10 years old, Momma found a nice rental house. At last, we had a place where she thought we might settle down for a while. That's what she thought.

What happened one night, I swear, I was just following my sister Melinda. We was bored. We both knew my mom kept a pile of newspapers in the utility room. Momma would use them for everything, wrapping food, gifts and school projects. So, Melinda and me, we thought, "Let's see what's up that we can do with that."

As I said, it was Melinda who was messing around with the newspapers. She would light the newspaper, and then she'd blow it out. Then she'd blow it out, and then set it back on fire. I seen her do it, and then I did it. I'm her little brother, so you know, I'm going to do the same thing. Well lo' and behold, it almost burned me! So, I got scared, and I threw the newspaper in the trash. And, yes, the other side was still lit. It was still lit.

Next thing I know, I looked around the room. The whole house was on fire. I heard screamin' from my other siblings. Melinda and I started screamin' for everybody to get out. It was like a movie scene. One at a time, they was running out that door with smoke pouring out.

Finally, everybody was almost out the door. Then came Momma. Right before my momma hit that last step, the whole house blew up. Thanks to God she wasn't hurt. I was so glad, but I was even happier she didn't know why the fire started.

The whole family, all nine of us, we had to stay with the neighbors. I don't know how Momma talked them into it. We stayed with them neighbors for two months. Finally, Momma decided we needed a break from Muncie. She wanted to look for greener pastures and have some new scenery. She was tired of seeing what was going on in Muncie and wanted another life. So, I guess Momma thought, go big or go home! We just all up and moved to California. I didn't even know where California was. I was born in Muncie. I had to leave all my friends and all my cousins.

I knew that I had family in California. My Aunt May, my cousin LaMonte, my cousin Monica and my cousin Lara all lived there. Lara was married to Muff, and he was California stylish. He wore suits and a big hat. We called him Muff McCoy.

Once we got to California, I realized it wasn't so bad. We had new scenery and new food. Palm trees lined the street. We discovered ramen noodles. They didn't have those in Muncie. I swear my family introduced Ramen Noodles to Muncie.

Me and my siblings and cousins there, we played foosball. I couldn't say "pop" no more, so I learned to say, "soda." We had break dancing competitions. Those were big everywhere in California. My cousin won a big one.

I went to a nice school, Dover Elementary. It had a lot of the new things on the playgrounds. They used recycled tires to make swings and jungle gyms. I loved playing on those. One plain and simple day, I was out having a good time with my friends playing foosball. Then, I decided to go play fort in a pile of tires built up into four walls. Suddenly, it got real quiet. I looked up, and all my friends had left. I didn't know why. I suddenly realized I was out there all by myself.

Through the quiet, I heard voices. I saw them coming in bright colored jackets. A bunch of guys was dragging one other guy along. They looked fierce. They was gang members. Some was Crips and some was Bloods. I can't remember who came out first. You know these California gangs; they was always feuding back in the early '80s (Hutson, et. al.. 1996). I crouched down in between the walls of tires. I was pretty sure none of them knew I was there.

I listened to them shouting louder and louder, and they were laughing. I can't tell you who did it first. The Crips or the Bloods ended up shooting this guy they was draggin.' They shot him in the head. I was right there. I could see in the spaces between the tires. I tried not breathing. I thought they could hear my heart pounding.

Those big guys, they probably shot that poor man about 16 times. And, I seen it. I seen it with my own eyes. I couldn't breathe. I was hiding, hiding, hiding. I was so confused cause they were all laughing. "Watch this guy jump," they was saying. "Watch him jump! We're gonna shoot him again!" It was like it was a plaything to them. And, I'm a young guy. I'm thinkin' like, "This is a body!"

As soon as they started walking away from that man bleeding on the playground, I got the opportunity, and I ran. I didn't stop running. I ran across highways. In California, you can get a ticket for jaywalking, crossing the highway where there's no green light. But I didn't care. I couldn't stop.

Finally, I got to our apartment. I ran upstairs and burst in the door. Momma said, "What's wrong with you?" I said, "Momma, I'm scared." I told her what I saw and said, "They're going to kill me!"

Right then, I heard a knock on my door. She looked out the door, and she knew. She didn't have to recognize them. She knew it was some Bloods. I heard the voice of one I recognized. I was just cold and shaking.

Those guys said to my momma, "Hey, can your son come out and play?" But thank God for Momma. She was smooth, man. She said, "He can't come out and play. You got to ask his daddy if he can come out and play. And his daddy ain't here now."

I was so scared that day. I can imagine…I can still see the face of that young man taking his last breath. I was learning stuff that I never should have seen. Momma knew she had to take care of me and all her babies. These greener pastures wasn't so green looking after all. So less than a year since we came to California, we left. We moved back home to Muncie, Indiana.

Hallelujah! Our small-town never looked so good.

Marwin in his Georgetown University jacket his freshman year at Muncie Central High School.

Marwin at 17 years old hugging his mother Martha on Mother's Day.

CHAPTER 4

BLOOD IS THICKER THAN WATER

"My brother Stevie, he was crazy in the head about his brother, Marwin"

After that experience in California, I think Momma and I had PTSD for a while, you know, Post-Traumatic Stress Disorder. I never could forget the face of that boy before he was shot. When we got back to Muncie, family seemed even more important. It was like we had to form our own gang to stay safe.

Even back in 1990, everyday people was still openly racist. Washington Park was one of those places where black kids wasn't supposed to go. But my family lived right along that park, and we wanted to play basketball on that court.

One afternoon when I was in middle school, my friends and me was playing basketball at that park. We was just out havin' a great time. Then, out came some big dudes. They was probably in high school. We didn't think much of it. We was all focused on the game. Those dudes didn't look friendly. But they came on up to us and asked if we wanted to play. I guess we was kind of shocked cause they was white. Sadly, this didn't happen a lot when I was growing up, getting asked to play with people of other races.

They said, "Why don't we play a tournament, boys. We can be IU (Indiana University) Hoosiers. And we'll play against you guys. You can be Georgetown players." IU was a predominantly white basketball team, and Georgetown University in Washington D.C., was a predominantly black team. Georgetown's Coach John Thompson had recently become the first African American coach to win a college basketball championship. So, we knew what they was implying, black against white. We was just like, "OK, man. Let's go!"

My friends and me, we was only in middle school. But we played hard. That game when it was over, boy, it was not close. We blew them out. Those guys wasn't happy at all. They turned red in the face. "OK, sons of bitches," they said. "Let's play again. We gonna get all of you niggers!" We're like, "Well, ok, white boys, keep on." We blew them out again. This happened over and over for hours. The sun was starting to set.

Finally, those guys got so pissed off, one of them grabbed a large rock. This big guy hauled off and slammed that rock into my old buddy Chad's head. He slammed that rock right into his skull. Blood was running down all over Chad's face.

I had been taking karate lessons for six years by then at the Multi, so I had a black belt. I wasn't afraid of them, but they was bigger and older than all of us. I couldn't fight so many of them. We couldn't whoop all them.

Those white boys started shouting, "Hey, don't you niggers ever come back to this park again." They wouldn't back off. They wanted to fight. Then someone on the block cracked open their door to see what was going on. Then, my biggest fear came true. They went and told my big brother, Little Stevie.

Now, this was bad. I knew better. I never told my brother Stevie nothin' cause he was crazy in the head about his brother, Marwin. He didn't play about that. Pretty soon, here came Little Stevie outside, big muscle-bound wrestling dude. He said real casual like, "Well, what's going on?"

Little Stevie recognized these guys. They played on the same football team as him in high school. I just about couldn't watch. Those boys started talking smart-ass like to Little Stevie. Holy shit! They wasn't prepared for what was coming. Boom! Remember these was not small guys. But it took Little Stevie no time to knock them all out cold, all six or seven of them.

Next thing I know, people was pouring outside they houses. My momma came running out of our house, and she was irate. She saw my friend with blood gushing out of his head, and she started screamin.'

Then, the police came. They was trying to make sense of it at first. But you know what happened? Those police didn't even come talk to us African Americans. They went right to the white males and the white parents. You know what those parents said? They said, "Officer, these niggers, they've been picking on our kids. All they do is come to Washington Park and pick on our kids."

The police never got our side of the story. They never even tried. They even called us that word. "You niggers, you got to get out of here," one officer said. "We gonna come back here in an hour or so. If you niggers is all still here at eight o'clock tonight, we're gonna take you all down to the station."

We never got to tell our part of the story. That's how it was back then. It was a real struggle. But you know the meaning of this lesson, don't you? Family is family. My family, oh we could fight! Ooohhh, we could fight! But you better not mess with my family. We take care of our own.

What about my brother? I couldn't help but be a bit proud. Who else has a brother like that? My Little Stevie fought for me. And in the end, he fought for himself too.

No one messes with Little Stevie.

1995 Muncie Central High School Varsity Basketball Team

Chapter 5

RESTORING MY SOUL

"I bought a brand, new pair of Doctor J's"

Muncie is a nice Midwestern town. It has a big university, a community college, a regional hospital and several well-known companies in finance and technology. But especially after plant closings in the 1990s, the distance between the haves and have nots got worse and worse. Downtown where the crime rate is highest, the rate of poverty is twice that of the rest of the community. People of color are only 10 percent of the community, but they make up almost half of those people in poverty. Thirty percent of the kids in town got free and reduced lunch at school (Muncie Weed & Seed, FY 2008). I was one of them. That is where I grew up.

The good part was, because the population of minorities was so concentrated, all cultures attended the downtown schools. We had African American, white, Hispanic, people from Asian countries, India and sometimes visiting students from Europe and Japan. We also had a broad socio-economic class. You had the preppy guy who had a mother and father who may be doctors. Then you had a guy with a single mother who worked at Borg Warner or New Venture Gear, the auto parts manufacturing plants, before they went out of business. Then you got me, and a lot of my friends, who didn't have nothing.

The bad part was that in addition to racism, different classes of people was prejudiced against each other. You know some white kids wasn't treated right. The way people thought was that we poor kids couldn't have what the rich kids had. We couldn't be the honors students.

As a black child at that time, we was frequently called "dumb little nigger." There's an ugly power with that word too for black people. In our history, that word was used to mean a low-down, dirty person. As kids, we heard that enough times, many of us started to believe it. We heard it enough many of us thought we was never gonna amount to nothing (Kellogg. 2018).

Even those who was supposed to protect us talked like that sometimes. You could tell some police officers was well-meaning. But other police would call us niggers and tell us to get out, saying we was in the "wrong place." They would see us out in Shedtown, a primarily white neighborhood, or at Ross Community Center where those kids went. They would call us names and say, "I'd better not see you out here ever again in my life."

Muncie schools had some beautiful and great teachers. Some good teachers was white, and some good ones was African American. But even at school, some teachers was bad news. Imagine that you was a kid and a lot of people in authority in your life called you a name like that. You hear that word over and over, how do you not start to believe it?

It was scary growing up watching your back. It was scary knowing we wasn't safe. Lots of young men was in fights. We got jumped. The white guys, they got jumped too. It was crazy. Craziness was going on all that time. Thank goodness for basketball and basketball coaches.

Two coaches was so significant in my life, I would not be the man I am today without them. Mr. Wilson (I never knew his first name) coached at Washington Carver Elementary. At that time, I was a small kid, probably only like about four foot three. But I was one of the fastest kids. Coach Wilson saw fit to give me some attention. When I think back to that time, he was probably the only one who built me up. He said, "Marwin, you can be anything you want. The sky's the limit for you."

Then when I went to middle school, I met someone who would really change my life. I knew every year in seventh grade the school had basketball tryouts. I always wanted to play on a school team, but I had never gone to try out for any sport before. I didn't have no money for uniforms, no good shoes. In fact, I had some holey shoes, and I'm not talking biblical. They were basically, you know, slip and slide. My momma got them from Payless Shoestore. That ain't no Foot Locker. They was some kid's all-white Pro-Tecs.

I decided no matter what I was wearing, I was going to try out for that basketball team. When I got to the tryouts at the gym, a bunch of kids was running on the courts. Some had those old Keds tennis shoes. Some had new Air Jordans. No one else had Pro Tecs like me. My shoes looked like what those kids had when they was five years old. Probably those white lame-ass shoes was passed down to me, but I tried not to think about that.

At tryouts, I put my whole soul into it. I played hard. Basketball meant everything to me. It was my way of getting away from trouble. It was my way away from stress. I put it all on the floor. Everything. That was my fantasy away from reality. All I wanted to do was to play basketball. When I was dribblin' and dunkin,' I could get my mind off the things that was going on at home.

By the end of the school day, I was so nervous, I started blowing spit balls in the back of the classroom. I was concentrating hard on my spitballin' you know, rolling them up tight, gettin' 'em good and slimy, and then spitting them out of the end of a straw.

Some wise-ass student went up and told the teacher I was gettin' those suckers all over the classroom. That teacher was mad and sent me out. I was so scared that night. I said to myself, "Marwin, what's wrong with you, man? You might not make the basketball team cause you threw them spitballs."

The next day, after I'd been up worrying all night, I ended up waking up late for school. They used to post the tryouts results outside the gym, the list with all the names of the players who made it on the basketball team. But I couldn't go see the list cause I came in late that morning. That whole day I was like, "Man, did I make the basketball team? Did I make the team?" Nobody knew, or nobody would tell me.

All the sudden, I heard a voice on the loudspeaker. The secretary called me down to the office. I was scared, but I went and got a hall pass. I thought they was calling me cause I did spitballs the day before. I thought to myself, "Man, I'm about to get in trouble. You know you didn't make the basketball team."

As I was sitting in the office, I had butterflies. You know, sometimes you're scared when you know something important's coming but you ain't sure what. Then, this presence entered the room. He was a big, tall white guy. I mean I wasn't tall, and this dude was probably about six foot three. He had a big booming voice. If I ever heard a big booming white man voice like that, it wasn't usually talking nice to me. He said, "Marwin... Mer...how do you say your name? I'm Coach Lafferty."

I tried to act tough, but I thought my voice came out kind of high and squeaky, "How're you doing?"

Right then, I seen that big smile. I tell you, at that moment, I knew this big dude was gonna change my life for the better. Coach Francis Lafferty became one of the greatest influences in my life. Everybody in Muncie knew him. He was a legend in teaching basketball to kids from all walks of life. And, he would teach them well. In all my childhood years, and throughout my adulthood, he was the one who really stuck with me.

Coach Lafferty said, "Well, Marwin, with the shoes you had on yesterday, I don't see how you played so well. You were slipping and sliding all through my try-outs. But I'm going to give you a pass on that part. I talked to the principal, and I talked with your mom. I want to go down to the Rex Store with you, and I want to buy you some brand new tennis shoes. To be on my basketball team, you can't be wearing shoes like that." I know my mouth was hanging open. I'm like, "Wow!" I think I mumbled, thank you.

We went down to Rex, and I bought my first real, brand-new pair of Doctor J's. I can still see 'em in my mind right now. They was leather, and they was awesome, man! And, you know what? From then on, from seventh grade all the way through high school, Coach Lafferty bought me shoes every year. Coach Lafferty made me know I was important enough to deserve new shoes. That man, my mentor, set an example for me that still affects me in my adult life. Thanks to Coach, I believed I could break it down on the court, just like Michael Jordan.

In my mind, I could hear the crowd shouting, "Maaarrwwiinn!" What I didn't know was, it wasn't the crowd that was calling. Someone else was trying to get through to me. But I didn't hear Him yet.

Muncie Northside Middle School 8th grade Football Team

Marwin playing on the Forty and Over Basketball Tournament, hosted by Muncie Black Expo in Heekin Park (2019).

CHAPTER 6

PATHS OF GLAMOUR VS. RIGHTEOUSNESS

"I was deep into this illusion that I had the glamourous life"

By the time I was done with high school, I had two lives. One life was in the drug game. The other was the one in basketball. The basketball life had real potential to make me the man I was meant to be. My trouble was, I didn't make the choice. I thought I could be the Most Valuable Player, the MVP, in both.

You see, in my part of the community, nobody made a living except on the streets. All I saw was poverty. And the only way to fight it was by selling dope. That was how it was back then. In my neighborhood, we kids was thinking we wasn't gettin' no higher education, no good jobs, and no real life. That created the haves and the have nots (Kellogg, 2018).

In my neighborhood, selling drugs was the normal thing to do. All my friends who was dope slingers had nice clothes and nice cars. I wanted the same things. That was survival. I was a product of my environment. I just didn't see myself going to college. I wanted to, but no one in my family went to college. I thought I had to sell drugs to survive. I didn't see people in my community do it any other way

So, for four years after I graduated high school, I was just living this dual life, selling drugs and chasing after women on one hand and making baskets on the court in the other. Almost every day, I was going partying and living the street life. And I believed I was the MVP! I believed I was the best drug dealer in Muncie. Everybody knew Marwin. I was called the Boss Player. I was very cunning. I was a very persuasive guy. I knew how to talk to people. I knew how to have you buy my product. I was deep into this illusion that I had this glamor life.

I was also careful. I knew the law of the streets. I never robbed nobody. I never broke into anyone's house. I knew if I just sold marijuana and pills in small amounts, if I was caught, all I would get was just a misdemeanor. I might get probation, but I would not get in too much trouble. I'm not stupid enough to sell cocaine. That is a felony. So, I just stuck to marijuana and pills, and I helped myself to them too by the way.

In my other life, my basketball life, I was tearing it up on the basketball court. Remember in the late 1990s how basketball wasn't just a sport? It was the pathway to the stars! Everybody watched the NBA. Michael Jordan was on fire. Bulls was winning the series again and again. That was when IU's coach Bobby Knight was winning games and throwin' chairs across the court (NBA History, n.d.).

Those was the years I ramped it up. You may not know me, but I was almost there at the NBA. I was a standout high school player. I led in rebounding for the region. After high school, I played in tournaments all over. Part of me really wanted that life in basketball. Part of me believed I deserved to live that way. I really wanted to be on that path of righteousness.

I played with a lot of guys that were on their way to greatness. Bonzi Wells, who played in the NBA, he and I grew up together. We was homies. He wouldn't get near my drug life, but he was my friend. Bonzi couldn't understand with my basketball moves why I was livin' the drug life. He'd tell me, "You need to stop hanging around them dudes, man. You have your talent."

In 1997, Bonzi and me played together at the Five Star Basketball Camps they had all over the country for youth. We had our own Dream Team from Muncie, the Park Townies. It was: Bonzi Wells; Chandler Thompson, a Ball State Alumni; and Jay Edwards and Charles Smith from IU. And, here go me!

It was a three-day tournament and scouts from colleges was going to be there from all over. They was from places like Indiana University, University of Florida, and good old MJ's alma mater, the University of North Carolina. Me and my team, we played and played, and we kept winnin' and winnin'.

That tournament was a turning point for me. I got some serious recognition for the first time, all on my own. I couldn't believe it. It was like I was dreamin.' They said I was MVP! I was on the way to being one of the chosen ones. I was so excited. I thought, "Wow, man. I really am big shit now!"

The next day after the tournament, the leadership was going to hold the awards celebration. I was supposed to go to that and accept my MVP award. But after all that basketball playing that night, I just wanted to run home, go to parties and bask in the glory. I just wanted to go rub it in the face of my homies. Marwin would be seen not just as the best drug dealer, but he would be known as the best basketball player too, boy! I could be number one in both lives.

I left that the tournament that night saying to myself, "No sweat, man. I will get back here in time in the morning." But I didn't make it back. I didn't make it to my own MVP celebration. I was still living in that illusion that I didn't really matter, and that the only way to make it was to sell those drugs. I thought that I wasn't worthy of being a basketball hero. To this day, and to anyone in leadership from that tournament who might be reading this, I am sorry. I really regretted it. I should have showed the respect I was gettin.'

Lookin' back, I believe that God, and even other people, believed in me more than I believed in myself. After that incident, I would never have expected God would try to bless me again. But He did.

In 1998, Bonzi and the guys and I was still playin' together. I won MVP again that summer at the Bobby

Wilkerson Black Expo Tournament in Anderson, Indiana. I made 54 points and 26 rebounds.

The next week, our dream team played at the Indianapolis Pro Summer Leagues. Now that competition was a big deal every year at Washington Park in Indianapolis. We played game after game after game. And I was on fire, man. I was fast. I was quick. I wiped it up. Little Old Marwin. They called me the Fire Marshall. I put fires out on the other team. We made it to the championships.

So here was me, Bonzi, and these other well-known dudes. We was just a Muncie, Indiana team, and we was goin' to play a championship game in front of all these recruiters from across the nation and even overseas. Some of these guys represented feeder leagues that essentially groomed players for the NBA.

So, me and these NBA future stars, we was gettin' ready for that championship game. And I about lost it when I found out who was going to be with us on the court for the championship game. They was my heroes. It was the team from the University of Kentucky that had just won the NCAA championship that year. I was supposed to play them? I'm like, "Man, you are shittin' me!"

As we got started, we was all supposed to shake hands with the opponents. All the UK guys was respectin' my teammates. They knew something about Bonzi and them. They was smilin,' shakin' my teammates' hands and saying, "How're you doing today? What's up?" But not to me. They was not smilin' at me. They just said under their breath real quiet, "Hey," and gave me a little fist bump. I said to myself, "Ooooh, boy. Whoa no, motherfuckers. You shouldn't treat me like that."

They had just lit a fireball. I got mad. I got angry! I was like, I'm about to put it on now! What they didn't know was, they should not have tried to put me down. That just put me into this zone where I had like this killer instinct for winnin.' I wasn't gonna put up with no disrespect. So, I ripped it. I was fast. I was down low. I did posts. I did long shots. An 18-foot-long shot was nothing. I got the ball and rolled it on down, faded away like Jordan, then rebounded and dunked like Dennis Rodman. And would you know it? I ended up getting 50 points and 23 rebounds in that game, and I got the MVP of that tournament, again. After that, everybody from different colleges and cultures was comin' up askin', "Do you play college basketball?"

I would say, "Not yet!"

That day I got invited to play the next month at the United States Basketball League (USBL), the men's minor league, which was like a development franchise for the NBA. I went up there and played. I made the final cut. I even got invited to play at Indiana State University. When I heard that, I just bawled. That was like my dream. I also got calls from the University of Florida, the University of Miami of Ohio, and North Carolina State.

Then, a few weeks later, I got the big call. The NBA Charlotte Hornets wanted me to come down to North Carolina and try out for their professional team. Their recruiter had seen me play at Washington Park and then again at the USBL. I was to go down to Charlotte on the second day in October of 1998. I will never forget that day if I live. But there was two long months before that try out, and those demons was swirling around me. It was like I was ready for the three ghosts of Christmas. But they was only shadows, and I wasn't payin' attention, so I didn't see what was comin'.

Muncie Indiana Black Expo, Basketball Tournament, Most Valuable Player and 1ˢᵗ Place Championship trophies (1998).

Marwin with his father, Michael Hall, on the porch of his grandmother's house in Muncie (2015).

CHAPTER 7

MY FATHER CAME FOR HIS NAME'S SAKE

"Put that motherfuckin' gun down!"

God was about to throw down His last warnings to save my life. He chose some strong messengers, man. Sometimes God's messages come from the people you least expect.

My daddy, Michael Hall, left me when I was seven years old. He was hooked on heroin. He said he didn't want me to see him like that when I was growing up. So, he moved to Detroit, Michigan and was in and out of prison. Even though I acted like I didn't want nothin' to do with him, every kid who has a daddy that's missing knows how much it would mean to have a dad active in your life.

I called him Pops. He'd come to Muncie to see me now and then. He'd write to me. I'd write back sometimes, and sometimes not. I thought I hated my father back then. I just knew he was never there. Never came to watch me run track. Never threw a ball with me in the yard.

As a young kid, I thought I didn't have nobody to tell me, "Marwin, you could be anything you want to be out of life. You could be the best. You could graduate from Ball State University." I also didn't think about no consequences. Kids don't think about that. That's why they always in trouble.

After high school, I stepped up my slingin' drugs. By age 22, I was a single dad with two kids. I thought I had the best of both worlds. I loved the party life. I wanted to go kick it and have a good time. Like a lot of young people, I even used the "N word."

You know what was ironic? Pops was proud of me. I had all the women, all the money and a nice, canary yellow colored Cadillac. I was paid for selling drugs with Cadillacs and triple gold bars. From where Pops was at, that looked like the good life to him, too. But my daddy and me was about to get a dose of reality.

By that time, Pops was almost one of my gang buddies. My guys and me in Muncie was the Dogg Pound Gang. Sometimes when Pops was back from Detroit, he would be out kickin' it with us. See, I really loved my father. Even though I hated how I grew up without him, he was my father.

I believe God brought my Pops back to me in Muncie for a purpose. Lookin' back, I see how my Heavenly Father sent my earthly father to try to get me out of the drug life, whether Pops realized that was his job or not. Pops was with me that night in the summer of 1998 when the first of the last three warnings came from God. We was hangin' out on the street with one of my cousins. Outta' nowhere, this guy come out with a chrome pistol and stuck it in my cousin's face. I guess my cousin owed this guy's friend some money. This bad ass with the chrome was here to collect.

Before I could stop myself, big old me, I was up in this guy's face. "Put that motherfuckin' gun down, you bitch-ass nigga!" That was what came out of my mouth. I had jumped in front of my cousin and between him and the gun. I kept yellin' at the guy with the pistol in his hand, "You ain't gonna shoot nobody tonight, mother-fucker. You ain't gonna shoot nobody tonight. You keep talkin', motherfucker, I'mma smack the shit outta you."

My Pops, he saw what was happening and jerked up like he was on fire. He was in shock seeing me, his son, standing in front of a gun. He pushed me out of the way and said, "You crazy, Marwin!" That was when my daddy realized that this life for me, being the number one drug dealer, it had a price. That price was my life.

In my mind, that was God's Hail Mary for me. He used my Pops, one of the only people who could reach me, someone who came from the same side of the tracks and had as many sins to carry, to try to get me out before someone took me out. God sent my Pops to see if he could get me the message that I better change, or my life was in danger.

I remember I could see it in my Pop's eyes that night, the sadness and fear. It was too late. Not even Pops could change me. I thought I was invincible, and I refused to listen. The next time the evil shadow crossed my life, it was even worse. It was Little Stevie. My big brother, the big wrestler, and my protector since I was a kid.

Little Stevie got shot.

Coach Charlie Titus from the University of Massachusetts in Boston with Marwin Strong at an NCAA basketball game in Indianapolis (2006).

Coach Titus, and his wife Paula, with Marwin (2006).

CHAPTER 8

THE SHADOW

"You gotta come now, Marwin,
Stevie is bleedin' out all over the floor!"

The day my cousin almost got shot seemed like a dream to me. I remember I said to myself, "It can't be that hot in Muncie, man This is small town America. I'm an MVP on the streets and on the court. I'm hot and in charge of my own life. I just gotta' try to move on." I thought I was still a success. I was out makin' money. I always looked good. Those demons was seductive man.

One night that same summer, my brother Stevie and I was out drivin'. I was still ridin' in my Caddie with my jams. My woofers so loud the cars next to me was jumpin' off the hot pavement. Whoo-ee!

We stopped to sit out on the hood of my car and drink some Hennessey. We was havin' a great time the two of us. After a while, some of Stevie's homies came drivin' by with their triple Ds, those nice Cadillac rims. Those guys was yellin' at him to go to a club in Anderson. Anderson was about 30 miles away, closer to Indianapolis. Sometimes we had more action there, but the small town had more of the city life influence. One of them influences was a rival gang. Muncie gangs wasn't always welcome in Anderson.

It was my turn to have a bad feeling. I begged Little Stevie. I said, "Why don't you just stay here with me. We chillin' and havin' a good time." But Stevie was like me. Or, I was like him. Invincible, he thought. Anyway, he got in that car with them.

A few hours later, I got a call. It wasn't a good call. One of those guys who took Stevie to the bar in Anderson was shoutin' to me on the phone, "You gotta come now, Marwin! Stevie is bleedin' out all over floor. Don't know how many times he was shot. You gotta come now, man."

"I'm gettin' the crew; we're comin,'" I said and told my best homies from Muncie to go get a stash of guns we had and meet me at the club. We never usually used 'em. But I guess they was there for nights like that. Once again, God had my back that night. Some cops pulled my guys over on their way to Anderson, and they had to throw the guns out the window before the cops saw them. The cops kept the guys long enough that they couldn't get to the bar to start a fight.

I didn't know my friends was stopped by the cops until later. When I got to the club, I didn't see nobody I recognized. When I said who I was to the bartender, this one girl came up and said she had seen it all. She told me everything. Stevie had been drinkin' heavy and felt sick. Bro' needed some air, so he went to the parkin' lot to chill out in the back of his friend's car.

Like I was afraid of, the Anderson gang got word that Stevie's Muncie crew was at that club. So, a few of them guys went out into that parkin' lot to jack the Muncie gang's car. They opened the door to start climbin' in. They saw Stevie sleepin' in the back of the car and demanded he get out so they could steal the car. Stevie got up and took off running toward the bar as fast as he could. But those Anderson guys, they shot him three times while he was runnin,' once in his ankle and twice in his chest.

I don't know how Stevie did it, but he was a strong man. After those guys took off in the car, Stevie dragged his ass, bleedin' from the ankle and the chest, all the way from the parking lot into the door of the bar. Then, he passed out on the floor. Just so happened a nurse was at the club that night. Another gift from God I believe. That nurse got up on him and started putting down pressure especially on the wounds on his side. That's what was going to kill him. I guess the nurse went with him to the hospital. I know she saved his life.

The girl from the bar said to me, "You got to get to the hospital fast. I don't know if he made it or not. They already taken him there." So, I got in my car and floored it. It's a wonder I wasn't pulled over. I beat that ambulance. I made it to the hospital and was waitin' there in the ER's front door when the paramedics brought Stevie in. He was a mess. He looked dead already.

I didn't know God then. I didn't grow up knowing Him. But I did pray that night. I cried and I prayed for Stevie like my own life depended on it. The next days was touch and go. Stevie was in and out of consciousness. But my man, he was a wrestler. Remember, no one messes with Little Stevie.

It took 21 days. But eventually, Stevie was out of the hospital. He was alive. I knew very well he almost lost that battle. What I didn't see was that, for me, this was the final warning. It was a warning to all of us, to me, to Little Stevie and others in my family. Get... out...of...this...life! Eventually, Stevie did get out. I'm so proud of him. He's in the corporate life now.

I believe now that God was trying to save us. God knew we was all in a fight to the death with those demons. We was His children. No matter what we'd done, He wanted us. God valued us. He wanted us to do some good in this world, and He sure was fighting against Hell, for us. If you look at life that way, it makes much more sense, don't it?

First my cousin, now Stevie. Who was next? God knew, and He tried to warn me. Next, those demons was coming for me.

"The Dogg Pound Gang," from left: Sweets, L.A. and Boss Player (Marwin) at Parkview Apartments (1997).

CHAPTER 9

THE VALLEY OF DEATH

"I was about to die"

After Stevie almost died, once again, I thought about getting out of the drug life. That was when my basketball career seemed like it was takin' off too. But still, I had no confidence. I didn't know at that time that God thought I was worthy of saving. It seemed to me it was easier to escape with the drugs I was sellin' than it would be to get out of the drug life. I never did no heavy drugs. Never used a needle. But I did weed, and I got into the pills, prescription opioids, like soma and valium. Sometimes I took 'em both at the same time. Then, I would have some weed with it.

Just a few weeks after Stevie got home from the hospital, I was out at another party. I was high on life, man. I was going to Charlotte, North Carolina in a couple of months to try out for the Hornets, an NBA team. So, I was ridin' that wave, that high, feelin' hazy headin' into the club. I look back and think, it was kind of eerie. The lights was red, and it was smoky and hazy inside. That bass sound from the music was beatin' in my chest. The rumble vibrated through the treads of my shoes. I was blowed and drinkin' too.

The girls they always liked me. I treated 'em well by comparison with other guys. This girl she came and asked me to dance. I can still hear that song, I was jammin' to that song by Juvenile, "400 Degreez."

While I was dancin', I remember seeing these guys I knew all talkin' and laughin' around this table. I was thinkin,' "They probably impressed that I'm so dope and goin' to the NBA." So, it made sense when they said to me, "Hey Boss Player, we wanna buy you a drink!" They handed it to me. I'm thinkin,' "That's cause I'm a popular guy, you know."

After I chugged it down, it struck me as odd. I felt like I was punched in the chest. When I drunk it, I thought I heard those guys sayin' something to me. Was it them, or was it the music? It didn't make sense. They was sayin,' "Die slow, motherfucka.' Now, yo' gonna die slow.'" I did not understand what they was sayin.' I thought that, yeah, I feel funny, but it had to be the music. I was just high.

Most of the time when you drink, there's that burning feeling of alcohol running down in your chest. Usually it goes away real quick. This time, I noticed that feelin' just wouldn't go away. It kept burnin' and burnin.' I tried to dismiss it. But as the night went on, I was thinkin,' "What in the world happened to me? What is going on?" I thought maybe I ate somethin' funky. Something wasn't right. I left soon after that.

The next days, I started feelin' like I had ringworms itchin' all over my hands. My hair started fallin' out. I was losin' weight real fast. I couldn't eat anything. I went to the doctor. He said, "Oh, don't worry. It's just a little common cold." That common cold didn't go away. I felt worse. I was vomiting and it was a brownish color (Ahmad, 2020). So, I went to another doctor. He thought it was the flu and bronchitis, and he gave me antibiotics.

I got so I couldn't walk very well. I needed help. So, I went to several hospitals in Muncie, in Anderson and finally one in Indianapolis. I stayed in that Indianapolis hospital for a couple of days, and they did all kinds of tests. But still after that, they didn't really know what was wrong. I didn't want to just lie there in the hospital for no reason. So, I refused to stay any longer. I figured I had been sick that long, what difference would it make? It had been 31 days I had lived like that on a downward slide.

I could not take care of myself, so I was livin' at home with my momma. When I got home from that hospital, boy, she was mad. She could not understand why I didn't want to stay and find out what was wrong with me. Since Momma and I was having a little feud over that, I started packin' up to stay with my sister that night. I went into the bathroom to wash my face one more time before I go.

I was standin' there looking at myself in the mirror. I didn't even recognize myself. I was only 125 pounds on a six food three frame. I said to my momma from the bathroom, "OK, Momma. I'll go. I'll go to church. I'm ready to change my life." I prayed in my head. I said, "God, if you ready to have me, I want to come to you." I guess He heard me. SMACK!

The last thing I remember was looking at my own sweaty face in that mirror. My family told me later that right after I said that about going to church, they heard a bang, and Momma found me on the bathroom floor having a grand mal seizure. My brother Michael was there, and he rushed over and scooped me off the floor. It was effortless to him cause I weighed so little. They all rushed me to the local hospital, Ball Memorial.

I ended up gettin' rushed into the ER and real fast they had eight tubes stuck into me. I had a trach in my neck. That means they cut a hole in my neck so I could breath. I had a PEG tube in my stomach, which is somethin' that feeds you directly into your stomach when you can't eat. I couldn't eat. I couldn't swallow. I didn't know where I was or what I was doing there. I didn't know who everybody else was. I couldn't remember names.

For months, I was in and out of consciousness. I didn't know how to walk, and I couldn't talk. The doctors kept tellin' my Momma not to get her hopes up. "We do not have good news," they said. They told her I was gonna die. Momma told me later one doctor came in and said, "Even if he does live, this young man, he's not going to be able to walk again. He won't be able to talk again. He will be a vegetable."

But I hung on. They kept doing tests and finally diagnosed me with what they called systemic lupus. They put me on 23 pills. But my kidneys started to shut down. They had to operate to flush out the kidneys. When I woke up the doctors said, "Marwin, we know what's killing you. We found two tablespoons of iodine in your kidneys (Ahmad et. al., 2020). We could not flush it out. So, we are putting you on an aggressive regimen of dialysis and chemotherapy. We are going to try to save you. But you may never live on your own again."

I thought back to that night at the club. It had to be those guys who got me a drink. I'm not gonna tell you what it was those would-be killers used to get iodine in my drink that night. I don't want to give nobody any ideas. Turns out iodine used to be popular in suicides which is crazy cause dyin' like that is slow and it's painful, man (Ahmad, 2020). I didn't know nothin' about it. But the guys at the club that night did. Then It came over me. Those guys tried to kill me. They may have already killed me. I wasn't sure I was gonna make it yet. But I was ready to fight like hell. I was finally ready to fight for myself as hard as God was fighting for me.

These doctors and nurses at the Ball Hospital, man, God was working through them. They didn't give up on me. They did ten rounds of chemotherapy for my kidneys. They did the dialysis. They knew, if they couldn't get my kidneys functioning right, I would be on dialysis for the rest of my life. If I lived very long, that is.

Eventually, I went into a coma. I was in a coma for a month. I had a drain for leakage on one side of my brain for a bleed. My momma said the doctors came in one day after I had been out for a while and said, "This young boy's about to die." They started taking tubes off me. The doctors literally said, "Get the obituary laid out. His kidneys are failing. All his organs is failing. He has a leakage in his brain. He's going to die."

You know how people in situations like this have visions? I had an out of body experience. A lot of people don't believe in Hell. Lemme tell ya. It's real. I've seen it. One day I was lyin' in bed in the dialysis unit, and I was barely conscious. I hadn't walked in weeks. But I saw myself move outside of my body. God came to me and told me to get out of bed. So, I followed Him.

When I walked with God out the door of the dialysis unit, all I saw was fire. I knew I was about to die. I remember it as clear as yesterday. God said to me, "You must follow in my footsteps. You need to walk with me all around this hospital hallway and follow the pattern of shapes in the floor." The hallway in the hospital had a pattern with geometric shapes in colors in the floor pattern. He said, "You must step only on those shapes. If you miss one, you will fall into the fire and be in Hell forever. Do not look either to your left or to your right no matter what they say to you."

Then, in my peripheral vision, I saw who he was talking about. They were in jail cells screamin'. Demons. Dead people. I had descended into Hell. I mean the real Hell. I could see from the corners of my eyes, with peripheral vision, the souls of dead people. Men were in fancy suits crying. I saw a doctor with his eyeballs cut out. Every race and age was there white people, black and brown people, men and women and even children. They was all screamin' at me trying to get me to look at them. They was in agony. I kept my eyes in front of me. And I remember walkin' slowly, slowly, and only on the shapes. I was doin' what I was told. I had to do what I was told. I couldn't go off and do what I wanted on my own anymore. I got the message.

Finally, I came all the way back around to my hospital bed and saw myself go back inside my body. The fire finally stopped. As I lay back in the bed, I saw what looked like a big ball of sunshine in the TV set in the hospital room. The Lord said, "Arise!" I knew I had died that day. But He brought me back cause I made the right choice, and I had work to do. I had to show love to Muncie and clean up what I messed up.

The nurses told me later, that while I was havin' that vision, I went completely nuts. I was pullin' out tubes from my arms and my sides. They had to tie me to the table and restrain my legs. They put mitts on my hands so I couldn't scratch myself or anyone else.

They told my momma I was goin' to be schizophrenic. They tried givin' me Haldol. You know how strong Haldol is? It's like a tranquilizer. It made my Soma's seem like aspirin. That was the lowest point in my life almost dying.

Finally, the hospital transferred me from the Intensive Care Unit to physical rehab at the hospital. I didn't know it then, but that rehab unit was going to be my new home for the next two years of my life. I also didn't know what my life was gonna look like on the other side.

Marwin in Dallas, Texas (2019).

CHAPTER 10

I WILL FEAR NO EVIL

*"They wasn't sure if whoever tried to kill me
would come back to finish me off"*

When I got wheeled into the physical rehab unit at
Ball Hospital in Muncie, nobody expected me to walk
out. In fact, they called in the nurse who was the last
resort for patients who may never recover. At that time,
Jan Carter-Goldman had been a nurse for 40 years. She
had been a cardiac nurse and a nurse in intensive care.
She was the one the hospital called in for patients with
no hope. No other nurses wanted these cases. They gave
Jan a choice if she wanted to take me. Thanks be to
God, she did.

Nurse Jan was about my momma's age and was like
a second mom. Just like my momma, she was tough.

When I first came in, Nurse Jan said I was near death. I couldn't talk, and I couldn't walk. The doctors said I would never walk again, and that I would be in a wheelchair the rest of my life. But Jan didn't believe that. She was my angel.

Jan didn't know the whole story, but she knew I had been in the drug life. I was so weak that I couldn't protect myself. So, she tried to be there all the time to protect me. In addition, police officers stood guard outside my bedroom all the time. They wasn't sure if whoever tried to kill me would come back to try and finish me off.

The police never did find out who spiked my drink. I had memory problems, so I could only be speculatin.' People I thought was there at the club that night would say it wasn't them who spiked my drink. Others came and told me who they thought it was, but I never really knew. In the end, I kind of thank those guys who tried to kill me for doing that. It forced me to make big positive changes in my life.

When my brain started rememberin' everything that happened, the reality of what I'd lost hit me hard. It had been more than two months since I started gettin' sick. I was supposed to go to North Carolina to try out for the Charlotte Hornets in October. It was

November now. I missed it. I had missed my try out for the NBA when I was unconscious. It crushed me that I missed that opportunity. Instead of heading to the NBA, I almost died. It was overwhelming.

I had therapy two times a day. I went to occupational therapy and speech therapy. We started slow. I was so shaky. I had to be strong-willed cause many times I wanted to give up. I even wanted to die sometimes because I was in so much pain and agony. I would sometimes be mad at myself, and I started to get down on myself.

Nurse Jan didn't just do physical therapy with me, she also did mental therapy. I really needed to believe in myself again. Jan said she could just tell that I had been through a religious conversion, and that she saw good in me. She said, "Marwin, we're gonna get you going again so you can play basketball. You are so lucky, Marwin. People don't survive with that much iodine. It just kills your organs including the heart and the kidneys. Your body is not made to ingest that. You are lucky to be alive. You got to get up and do this, Marwin, because you're going to do big things." To this day, she calls me her "miracle child."

Thankfully, Jan was strong even though she was only about five feet tall. She only came up to my waist. When I stood up for the first time, she just kept watchin' and watchin' as I got taller and taller. "Okay. Well, here we go!" Jan said to me, "It's just you and me, kid. If you go down, I go down. We're in this together." When I wanted to give up, Jan was brave and persistent. She never gave up on me. One day at a time, she said, and then helped me get in one more step.

Speech therapy worked a whole other kind of memory muscle. Jan showed me how to hold my hand over the hole in my neck left by the trach tube. This helped me be able to make a noise with my vocal cords so I could learn to talk again.

My brain had to rewire itself to form language. People sometimes laugh at me now because I can speak properly, like British English, real proper. Then there are times when Ebonics comes out of me. Ebonics are those slang words I grew up speaking, part of my culture, and that's a good thing. I still want to recognize my culture and drugs ain't gonna be a part of it. So, the doctors said, I ended up with the Ebonics part of my brain from my other life reconnecting with my proper English brain that I learned in the hospital.

I was in rehab in the hospital for two years. Police was still all over there. Even though Jan was amazing, being at the hospital all those days and nights was lonely without my family. When my mother and sister couldn't come, like when Indiana blizzards hit, I felt alone. Other than Jan, I didn't trust the nurses. I didn't trust nobody. I felt weak and alone. Finally, I would just start saying, "Jesus, Jesus, Jesus, Jesus." Next thing I knew, it would be five o' clock in the morning, and the nurses would wake me up saying, "Marwin, we got to take your blood." I started building up my faith. I was making progress.

Then one day God and my momma sent a miracle. I got a call from Momma's brother, my uncle, Wallace Johnson. He knew about my basketball playing, and he wanted to help me get a second chance in life. Wallace was a standout basketball player at Ball State and had coached all over the east coast for years. At that time, he was at Brandeis University in Boston (MIT, 1997-1998). And he had a friend he thought could help me out. That friend was Coach Charlie Titus, from the University of Massachusetts in Boston. When he told me that, I could hardly believe it. I knew that name.

Coach Titus was considered the Founding Father of University of Massachusetts in Boston Athletics. He grew up in the projects just like me. He helped establish the Little East Central Conference for Division Three teams. And he led UMass Boston to the team's first NCAA Tournament (Aguiar, 2014).

My uncle and I talked a long time. I told him, "I want to find another way in life and get off the drugs and the streets. I want to play basketball more than anything when I get out of the hospital." After a lot of talking back and forth, my uncle said, "Marwin, if you really want this then you need to put all your work into it. Write a letter to Coach Titus and send it to me. Tell him all the details about what you've been through. I'll give that letter to him."

So, I wrote Coach Titus a letter. And, you know what? Coach Titus called me in the hospital. Coach asked how I was doing. He asked, "How much do you weigh?" And I said, "I'm almost to 190, man. I'm looking good." OK, so I weighed about 123. I was almost at 190. I would get there.

Then, Coach asked me, "What do you want to be the rest of your life?" I said, "I want to play basketball." He asked me to come to Boston and show him I could play...in July. It was January. That was in just seven months. I'm in the hospital. I couldn't even walk!

After we talked, I immediately called the guy in physical therapy at the hospital. I said, "I want to go back down there to the PT room. Now. I'm about to go try out for UMass Boston basketball team in July." The physical therapist thought I was crazy.

I focused like never before. I started to have faith in myself. Physically and mentally I started to rip myself up. I started running in water and pumping iron like my life depended on it. The physical therapist said, "Man what is wrong with you, dude?" I said, "You got to understand, man. I got to get this right. Even after I missed my chance in Charlotte, I'm still going to the NBA by way of the NCAA!" So, this was a test for me.

When you are in the game…they ain't no bottom to the game. In the drug game anything could happen. Sure, it was glamorous sometimes. But I never saw nobody get a 401k sellin' drugs. Guys would rob you or kill you so they could be on top. You had to watch out for both sides, the police and the gangs. It was part of the game. There are only two ways to leave the game. You would end up dead, or you would end up in prison.

Which game was I gonna play? Was I going to live? Or was I going to keep playing the game?

PART II

INTO THE LIGHT

From back left: Marwin's son, Dalvin Strong; grandson Braven Strong; Marwin Strong; son, Zion Strong and daughter, Malea Strong (2019).

CHAPTER 11

THOU ART WITH ME

"Marwin, there's another way"

The night before I left the hospital, Nurse Jan let me have my family over for dinner in a special, secret apartment they had at the hospital. She must have spent nearly 200 dollars of her own money to buy us all the best steak. It was a beautiful spread. It was one big party, man! But it was also important because I could show that I was finally ready to start living outside the hospital. Although I was weak, I was talking and walking again on my own. That proved I could make it. Finally, I was discharged.

I will never forget when I came back to visit Jan at the hospital months later. I remember walking down that long hallway toward her, toward that place where

I used to walk around and around every day. When she saw me, she just had a fit! I was in street clothes, walking tall. We had a big reunion hug. When I see Jan today, I always give her a big hug and call her "Mom-MAH!" I still consider Nurse Jan as a part of my family.

I wanted to keep my word to Jan, and to God, to maintain spirituality and faithfulness in my life. But it was hard on my own. Those lonely days and nights in the hospital, I read the Bible constantly. I basically taught myself about the Word. I started having encounters with God. I had trouble not beating myself up and moving forward. He spoke to me and said, "Marwin, there's another way." So, remember that promise I made to my momma before my seizure put me in the hospital? I saw it through.

One Easter Sunday, Momma took the whole family to the Greater New Life Worship Center in Indianapolis. The pastor there, Alvis Bond, and his leadership team welcomed me with open arms. They all professed that day that I would be healed mentally, spiritually and physically.

Pastor Bond said, "Marwin, are you going to give your life to God? If you come up here and dedicate your life to Him today, you will become a whole new creature. You can have a whole new life. The old things will pass away. You are a miracle, son. And you are going to testify to the world."

That moment was a miracle for me. I realized I could be forgiven if I repented and asked for a new life. But changing into this new person did not happen all at once. It took time. There was ups and downs. When I went through my lowest points, I would always go back to that time in my mind when I was in the hospital praying to Jesus to save my life. I would think, "Marwin, you almost died. This is nothing." No matter what obstacles came in the way, I got up and kept on going.

My faith started to give me energy. I was happy. I was excited. I realized any time you go through adversity, any time you try to change something, you're always going to have some depression. That's because your old mind and body are going to have that resistance to change. So, to change internally, you have to change your daily habits.

After I got out of the hospital, I played basketball regularly, just like I would eat a meal. I trained hard. I always kept that faith. I would hear that voice inside me again and again. "This is nothing. You almost died, young man, and you done got through. Now this situation you're in now. You know it's going to come to pass. You, Marwin, are going to be alright. There's a better life after this."

That summer, I went up to UMass Boston and played basketball for Coach Titus. I showed up for that tryout. Yes, I was back to a healthy 190 pounds, and I made the basketball team. For me, that was the culmination. I was like, "Yes!" I played basketball on the UMass Boston team that fall. It was hard. I made good plays, and I made bad ones. I was gradually getting better, and I loved it. I had a new place to live, regular food to eat. I went to classes and played ball. It was my dream life (Fitchburg, 2003).

But the change in my life was drastic. And I had so many conflicting demands that it was hard to juggle them all. I had to face not only challenges on the court but challenges of choices in my life. How was I going to be away from my kids back in Muncie? How would I make money for them? What kind of job was I going to train for? Even in the NBA, basketball doesn't last forever.

I would come back to visit Dalvin and Malea in Muncie every chance I got. And I was proud to tell them about my basketball career in college. I had changed so much. By that time, my kids were grown enough that they expected me to look professional. In fact, they had never seen me smoke and drink.

Later, in their lives, I would show my kids pictures of my days in the drug life. I would have guns in my hand, saggy pants on. On top, I'd have these all nice, Fubu clothes. My kids would say, "Oh Dad, that can't be you!" I had been hanging with gangsters. No, that was not what I wanted for my kids. I wanted to change my life, not just for myself, but for them, too.

It was heart-breaking when I had to fly back to Boston and leave my kids in Muncie. As much as I wanted to be on the court, I couldn't help but be thinkin' of those kids at home. Their momma worked, so sometimes they would be home alone. That was just like I had to do when I was growing up. That led to some bad behaviors. I hated to think about that. Hopefully, they were only home alone after school for a few hours.

One day, I got a call from my son Dalvin at about five in the morning. He said, "Dad, nobody's home. I need you to come home." I think they mom was around. She probably went and parked her car, I don't know. But these were my babies, man! I always had a close relationship with my kids, starting from an early age. I couldn't bear the thought of them growing up the way I did. I didn't want them to feel they had no shepherd. I didn't want them to end up like me.

I was at a crossroads in my life. And, I had to make a very tough decision. Did I want to stay in basketball and away from my kids? Or did I give up my dream of living the basketball life? If I go back to Muncie, will I end up back in old habits and dead or in jail? Or, can I return to Muncie to be with my kids and still change for the better? The decision was easy after all. I knew I wanted to live back home with them. I wanted to be there for my kids.

I went and told my coach, my hero Coach Titus. I needed to go home. I told him I knew I couldn't play basketball all my life. Basketball was temporary. My kids were there for life. They were my life. I said, "Coach Charlie, I got to get custody of my kids, man. I got to go home and take care of them. I can't have them home alone."

Coach said, "Marwin, I understand your kids are your main priority. But just do me a favor, son. When you go home, make sure you get a degree." I said, "You bet I will." Coach gave me a last gift. He flew me back home, and I got custody of my kids.

Many of my friends and family were shocked. It was mid-season, and I had worked so hard to get on a college basketball team. I was in the prime of my life, but I had a chance most people never have. I had lived my dream. It wasn't the NBA, but it was the NCAA. I went to school. I played basketball up there. Now that dream had to be done.

I knew what it was like to grow up without a daddy. I couldn't do that to my kids. I loved my daddy. I loved him so much that I didn't want him to see me make the mistakes he did. So, I made a choice to be a father. That is not giving up. That is not helplessness. It is power to make a choice, especially a tough one.

When I got home, I got that chance to save my kids and show them there was a better way. And you know what? I was able to help save my daddy, too. Pops came around from his drug life. When he saw me be saved, Pops said he wanted to get his life right, too. To this day, Pops is a praying man. And you know what? He allowed me to become a teacher to him. Any questions he has about the Bible, he still comes to me today.

People can hardly believe how Pops and me, we both turned our lives around.

So, if you asked me, "Why did you give it up, Marwin? Why did you give up on your dream to be in the NBA?" I didn't give up. I made a choice instead of letting life make a choice for me. I chose my kids and my family. I couldn't just think about myself anymore. I chose a better life for them and for me. I'll never, ever regret it.

From back left to right: Dalvin Strong, Malea Strong, Marwin Strong, Zion Strong and Samara Strong (2018).

Top photo, from back left: Zion Strong, Dalvin Strong, Samara Strong, Marwin Strong and Malea Strong (2019).

Bottom photos, left: Malea and Zion Strong (2019). Center: Samara and Marwin Strong (2019). Right: Samara and Marwin Strong (2019).

CHAPTER 12

GOD PREPARED MY TABLE

"What, you want me to put drug dealer on my resume?"

Coming home to my kids in Muncie was important, and it was the right thing to do. But it wasn't easy. I had to face the reality of living back in Muncie, a city that I loved, but where I had no experience except the drug life. I had to learn how to live in my hometown outside of the drug life. You know who was still there to help me? Coach Francis Lafferty.

When I came home, Coach Lafferty hooked me up with a job. It was like full circle, man. He still called regularly to check on me. He still wanted to help me.

He knew that it was hard because every day I had to make a choice of which life I wanted. I had to learn to have a regular job. I had never trained for that. It was hard living on the money I got. But Coach talked me through it because he didn't want me to go back to the drug game.

I remembered my promise to Coach Titus about going to school. Coach Lafferty also gave me the same dose of reality. He said, "Marwin, you need an associates and a bachelor's degree to stay ahead and be self-sufficient in this world." He was right.

My first job didn't last long because all the sudden the industry, which was legal and social work related, required a certification and years of training that I didn't have. Several workers were laid off including me. Just six months after coming home, I had no choice but to go on Social Security for a while. I could do that because I still had some disabilities from when I was sick. But I didn't want to be on Social Security. I wanted a job. I knew God had a plan. That plan had to include education. Where could I make money so I could go to school? All my resume had on it was that I had been a drug dealer, and that I did a short time playing college basketball out of state. As Dr. Martin

Luther King, Jr., said, I had to move forward in faith (Diaz, 2015).

At that time, I lived at Parkview Apartments. That was the projects where my mother and siblings and I lived when I was in high school. It was a real drug-infested area. I had sold drugs there. That's where I did all my dirt. At the same time, one of my brothers, Tyrone Heard from my dad's side, wanted to investigate living at another housing complex that was also part of the local housing authority. Tyrone was a single parent and had custody of his kids. I went with him to the management office at these other apartments to help him check it out.

When we got there, I saw a friend of mine in the office. I told her I was job hunting. She said, "Marwin, the Parkview Apartment Public Housing Manager's position is wide open. Why don't you try out for it?" I said, "Man, I appreciate it. But you know, I was a drug dealer. What am I going to put on my resume? What, you want me to put drug dealer on my resume?" She said, "I'll help you get that job. They need strong men like you, Marwin. They need strong men who have turned their lives around."

So, I applied. Then, I could not believe it when I got an interview. I met with Charles Weatherly of the Muncie Housing Authority. I was very honest with him about my past. I was proud to be an honest man. Charles was African American, and he oversaw hiring at Parkview. That made me happy to see him, an African American man, in a position of responsibility. And he was willing to talk to me.

I was sure with my history he wouldn't want me there, but I told him my story. He said, "Marwin, I'm hiring you on account of I believe you have changed, and you know something about life here. I'm hiring you because you can change this community around. We need a male figure that's 'been there done that.' I need someone who can show people it is possible to change. I can help you with the certifications you will need. I just need somebody out there who knows what it's like to live in this community."

As for the job? It was going to be a challenge. Parkview Apartments was a run down, 64 family complex. There were only 16 families living there when I started. I had to fill all those other apartments. I had to clean things up. So, I went back to the streets. But this time, I was on the other side. I had to confront people

I used to sell drugs with. These drug dealers were still on the block. I had to tell them, "Hey, I'm the new housing manager. I got to get families in here. You got to get off the block. No disrespect to you all, but I got to feed my family now."

I found out that my history was genuinely a benefit in that job. I had the street credibility. I had the reputation that I used to be "that guy." Because they respected me on the streets, those drug dealers just left the apartment complex. Next thing I knew, in about two months, the whole apartment complex was filled up with people.

At the same time, I knew just getting a job wasn't fulfilling my life's mission. I knew my community was hurting. I still saw kids on the streets using drugs, selling drugs and getting hurt. Every day in my office, I prayed. I said, "What can I do to change this environment?" I heard God in my head. He said, "Marwin, you need to start your own non-profit organization called the Fight Against Drugs and Violence."

I had the answer. It was on after that!

Enough is Enough Movement, left to right: Community activist Toddrick Gordon; Reverend Charles Harrison (Indianapolis Ten Point Coalition) and Marwin with television news crew from Channel 13, Indianapolis television news (2017).

CHAPTER 13

THE CURE OF GOODNESS AND MERCY

"When you're a black man you have two options; you can end up in jail, or you can end up dead"

Life was busy as the Housing Manager at Parkview Apartments. I was raising my kids. I kept going to church at New Life in Indianapolis and became a leader, first as a deacon and then as a youth pastor. Eventually, I also earned an elder's license so I could marry people and conduct funerals.

But that voice in my head kept coming back. It said, "Enough is Enough, Marwin. Children are dying in the streets. You need to do something about it."

God inspired to start a non-profit group, Fight Against Drugs and Violence. We set it up right, as a non-profit, 501c3 organization. A 501c3 status is a tax-exempt organization registered with the government.

The non-profit started by doing awareness, speaking to churches, clubs and handing out flyers out at community organizations. Then, I heard about the Ten Point Coalition in Indianapolis, a group of city, community and church activists who were patrolling the streets on the local TV news channels. These peaceful soldiers patrolled neighborhoods. They would go into homes and meet with people and families and encourage them to stop drugs. They would get people connected to resources to help. They had some imposing guys and gals in there, so just their presence discouraged violence. This group also worked actively recruiting businesses to hire former prisoners.

Awareness is one thing. Action is another. So, we got a group of community, government, non-profit and law enforcement representatives from Muncie who wanted to take it to the streets and created a movement Enough is Enough. You know, Muncie has the highest per capita giving rate in the state? We are fortunate here (McCann, 2019).

We met with the Ten Point Coalition in Indianapolis to ask for advice. The group, led by Reverend Charles Harrison, included city, church, government and law enforcement. They even got the former Indianapolis police chief, Rick Hite, to join. This group had an impressive record of statistically reducing drugs and violence in the inner city (de la Bastide, 2017).

When we met with Reverend Harrison and the other leaders, we asked lots of questions. "Do you think this will work in a smaller town like Muncie? What can we do to engage the community?" I shared the groups we had gotten involved already. They were impressed with our enthusiasm, and they agreed to help.

As soon as *The Star Press*, Muncie's local paper got wind of it, I'm telling you, the Enough is Enough movement came to life. The next thing I knew, it just blew up. It had a life of its own. We got groups and people contacting me who wanted to work together.

The Mayor of Muncie, the Muncie Chief of Police, the Delaware County Sheriff's Department and the Concerned Clergy (an active organization of primarily black churches) were all involved. We would have as many as 40 people working on this every weekend. Ultimately, we had 1100 people involved. We went in small groups to low income neighborhoods and reached out directly to people in their homes. We went door-to-door talking directly to people and talked WITH them, not AT them. We saw firsthand the pain people were experiencing.

With Muncie's poverty rate, many families were on food stamps. For hundreds of children free and reduced lunch at school was sometimes their only solid meal of the day. I could relate to that. People were frustrated. They didn't have the resources to improve their lives (MWS, FY 2008).

We explained to the residents, "We are not out here to get you; we want to help." If they were involved in drugs we would say, "You got to stop taking the drugs, stop the drinking and stop the smoking. You got a family. You can't sell drugs no more. You got to put the guns down. You need to think about the consequences of what you are doing. You are putting your life and your family members' lives in danger. I can tell you cause I did it. It all happened to me, too." We offered connections to resources and moral support.

With worse drugs came worse violence. At one time, Delaware County, was ranked number one in the State of Indiana for having the most meth labs. Young

11- and 12-year-old boys walked around with assault rifles, AK 47s, Tec-9s, shotguns. Where did they get those from? Sometimes we couldn't get the answers. We just ended up with more questions.

On the streets of Muncie, the drug violence became more ruthless. When I was young, even drug dealers followed a code of ethics to protect children. They would tell kids playing outside to get out of the way first. "There's going to be some shootings out here shortly," they said. "Get off the block!" We got it. Next thing they knew, we were gone! But that wasn't the code no more. Kids were getting caught in the crossfire.

When my kids were in high school, one of their classmates, Daiwan Walton, got shot to death in the crossfire of a drug fight. This was a 15-year-old child. Another young woman the kids knew was stabbed to death that same year. This was unreal. It was unacceptable. Children were dying in the streets of mid-town America (MWS, 2008).

The violence just cut at me, personally. Friends I grew up with were dying. These were men and women with children of their own. One of my friends got stabbed. Another one got shot to death. In one shooting, I knew both men, the one who got shot and the one who did the shooting. It proved to me you can't do anything without both sides. You've got to bring together neighbors and police. And you've got to work with both perpetrators as well as victims and their families.

In some ways, the worst tragedies were self-inflicted. Drugs and alcohol, caused by poverty, caused many people to give up and take their own lives. Most people would not expect this, but death rates from drug overdoses, and suicides from drugs are higher in rural areas than urban in the U.S. (U. S. Department of Health & Human Services, 2017).

A very, close friend of mine committed suicide. I had spent hours with him earlier that day. I tried to help him sit without drinking. I tried to get him to keep hope. I tried to let him know that I was living proof that jail or death were not the only choices. He was one of my best friends, but he died. People around me always died.

At the same time, I knew that the problem wasn't all individuals. In the big picture, drugs not only caused sickness in people, but they also caused disease in our justice system. Judges handed down sentences that were not right because the laws allowed bias. Why was it that a drug dealer who had been selling marijuana got more time than a sexual offender? I'm not saying it's right to smoke if it's illegal, but should that man involved with drugs get more time in jail than a child molester? The balance of justice wasn't there.

Government statistics show, racial discrimination was part of all of it with blacks almost three times more likely to be incarcerated (United States Sentencing Commission, 2017). I would see court cases where a white man convicted of a molestation charge might get probation, or maybe two years of house arrest. Then in the court next door, you had an African American guy who was caught driving while intoxicated. You know the sentence they handed down? They gave him 25 years. Go figure. Think how his mommy and daddy felt. Think about how African Americans felt when that happened. Why not just take his license? But, why make him pay 25 years?

And, why should all these black men and women be locked up for smoking pot when it's legal in half the country now? Don't smoke it if it's illegal. But why is it? I never saw anybody overdose on marijuana. The effects of those convictions were devastating for people who needed jobs. Even weed convictions could tank people's chances of getting a job. In turn, that increased the chances that person was going to jail. How was somebody going to avoid going back to prison without a job?

The roots for violent crime, and the feeling of being trapped and tolerating it, were also rooted early on in the education system (Theoheris, 2020). Dr. King called it the polite "white racism." The way history was taught created a mindset for blacks that put them down starting from a young age. Do you know what it is like to grow up as a black person in the regular classroom?

In my youth, we didn't learn about black history in school. My mother told me about it. In school we didn't hear about Martin Luther King, Jr, Malcolm X, Harriet Tubman or Rosa Parks. We didn't have the big "Black History Months." We didn't know about our culture.

History classes focused on slaves as victims and Black Panthers as the enemy. Hearing that over and over in school, we had the slave mindset drilled into us. We were told the white person always gets more than the black person. We were taught to be the "have nots" (King, Jr. 1968, reprinted 2018).

Growing up in the projects, there was such hopelessness. You didn't have a choice. You were gonna grow up to be a young baby daddy. You were gonna die at an early age by being killed. But you would never have a good job. You were gonna go to prison. That mindset taught in schools undercut students psychologically. I realized these stereotypes of African Americans weren't right when I got older and found out who I was. We needed to help other kids see that before it was too late for them (Kellogg, 2018).

Finally, the movement started to get some good results. To honor that work, I was voted as the *Muncie Star Press* Person of the Year in 2003 in our local paper. Members of the community voted to recognize the work of Enough is Enough. I was so proud of who I had become compared to where I had been. It meant so much that the community recognized this too. It proved an understanding that not only can you change to be a better person, others will see you for who you are now and not define you by your past.

It wasn't all about being Christian. You could be any religion or no religion at all. New life can start over again for anyone.

Dick's Sporting Goods blessed Texas Can Academy-Oak Cliff School Cougars basketball team with a gift of $1000 following their divisional championship (2020).

CHAPTER 14

THY ROD AND THY STAFF WERE MATH

"What do I do to get up out of here?"

After several years in the Parkview Apartments Housing Manager position, I had to keep my promise to go back to school and get a degree. Be careful what you pray for. What with the kids, the job, the anti-drugs and violence movement, and now with school, God's table got a bit too big for me. Living on faith, I did it anyway.

In 2007, I started an associate's in legal studies at Ivy Tech Community College. It was intimidating at first. I was a grown man back in a classroom. But the administration at Ivy Tech, the faculty, and many of the students, they supported me and encouraged me saying they were proud of me. I even ended up being in commercials with Ivy Tech. I got professional pictures. Pretty soon, those pictures started showing up on billboards all around the State of Indiana. These billboards are still there in some placees along the highway.

I figured I knew enough to have a leg up about the laws in court and on the streets. This may not sound like a good thing. But I was going to use that experience for good. I wanted to help others get off the streets, so I needed to know how to represent them. I knew what a class A felony was, a class B, C, or D felony. I knew what Indiana codes were. All my friends went through the prison system. I wanted to help people like them. I still went to visit them and went to court with them as part of my Enough is Enough movement. It all connected back to how I lived my life.

Ultimately, I wanted to go to law school and become a defense attorney. I wanted to help people who were like I was. I could explain to those who are in the judicial system that my clients were not the people that they thought. There is more to their stories.

I started having anxiety about getting it all done. "How am I going to get a bachelor's on top of the associates degree? Will I have enough persistence to get both?"

But God had a plan, and he knew how to reach me. He talked to me through my children. A lady came up to me one day at Ivy Tech and said, "I had a talk with your daughter about a way you can make sure to get your bachelors along with your associates degree. You could do it by going to Ball State right now while you're finishing up here."

Where I came from, Ball State University was like a castle on a hill. The thought of going there was a big deal to me. I'm like, "What? Ball State? Man, I'd love to go there!" There was just one catch. I had to pass math. I hated math. Math was just my worst. It was like kryptonite to Superman. I failed math like three times. And, I hated it. I hated it.

But I got help from a special program called Life-Steps at Ivy Tech. It helped me with math and resources outside of school. Coaches at the LifeSteps program helped students with math. It also connected students with community resources to get help with finances and social services support. It took all the study time and brain power I had to pass that math. I finally said, "I will pass it. Let's do it."

I just committed to it. Finally, I passed that math course! And I started classes at Ball State to start on my bachelors at the same time I was finishing up my associate's degree. In May of 2011, I graduated with my associate degree from Ivy Tech.

I really wanted a degree in criminal justice at Ball State instead of a generic bachelors. But I had been going to classes for years. I was working, going to school and still worked in leadership roles in the community. I was burnt out. I prayed for a way to do it all.

So, I went to the advisors at Ball State. I said, "Man, I'm burnt. But, I'm too close! What do I do to get up out of here?" They said, "Marwin, if you want a criminal justice degree, you're going to have to go another semester. But look, you already have your associate degree in legal studies. You can get two minors at Ball State with a general studies degree. One of those can be criminology." I'm like, "Yeah, let's do this! Let me get up on out of here."

I took some cyber classes that summer to get the last credits I needed, and I graduated in 2011 with a bachelor's from Ball State University. I made it! I did it! The undereducated drug dealer turned community activist now had a full plate of education to help make a difference. The Boss Player in the streets was now a Boss Player in life. Legit!

Ball State University Graduation Day for Marwin Strong on May 11, 2011.

After moving from Dallas, Texas in 2016, Marwin Strong maintained his work with the Enough is Enough movement in Muncie, Indiana. Here, he appeared at the Judge's Chambers in Muncie City Hall, to share with community leaders about his plans for renewed neighborhood outreach. Marwin was interviewed by Channel 13, WTHR, television news. Marwin and teams of people prepared to go door-to-door, three times a week, to share information with residents in high poverty neighborhoods. The teams gave residents information about free or affordable resources for drug rehabilitation, support for crime prevention and resources to help with utilities, food and other social services (2017).

CHAPTER 15

IN THE PRESENCE OF MINE ENEMIES

"Hey, boy!"

During my time as a student at Ball State, I got a new job opportunity as the first African American Delaware County Building Commissioner. It was kind of crazy. I had worked at the Muncie Housing Authority for almost four years. I got all kinds of accolades including being named the National Public Housing Manager. I was working on another certificate from the Muncie Housing Authority. When I thought about my life, I was satisfied, "I'm good here. This is what I'm going to do." But you know, God had other ideas.

Along came Bing Crosby. Who is that? Believe it or not, a private detective had been watching me to see if I would be a good fit for the job (Clipping Crosby, 2010). He had been watching me for six months. I didn't know who this guy was, where he came from, or what he did. But Crosby called me and said, "Hey, Marwin, you may not know who I am. But I have a job interview I am recommending for you."

Bing told me the county commissioners and judges needed a qualified person to be the Delaware County Building Commissioner and heard I might be a good fit. That was when I met Muncie lawyer and county commissioner John Brooke and Circuit One Court Judge Marianne Vorhees. Wouldn't you know, Judge Vorhees was also friends with Coach Lafferty's daughter. Hah! Here we go. That was the connection. "The coach's daughter, she brought your name up," Crosby said.

They told me they really wanted to have some-one at the county job who would be a stellar example and inspire others for leadership. They wanted some-one who had certifications and was qualified. As the building commissioner, I had to have knowledge of home construction and solid foundations to make sure structures of all kinds could pass federal codes. I would be responsible for getting homes and buildings up to code for HUD (Housing and Urban Development) to inspect the properties. It was critical so the county could get funding.

They knew I was experienced with that kind of responsibility. When I started managing at Parkview Apartments, the complex failed HUD inspections time and time again, partly because it was one of the oldest apartment buildings in the Muncie Housing Authority. We got "dinged" over things like crumbling sidewalks, or if the driveways didn't fit with the codes and use the right egresses. I was like, "Man, I'm tired of getting dinged!" So, we fixed those apartments up and got the HUD funding.

That job also led me to two of my great mentors in life. Commissioner Brooke and Judge Vorhees were very good to me. That job gave me more money, and it was a milestone. I was not only the first African American Delaware County Building Commissioner, but I was also the youngest to receive that position.

There were some ups and downs and merry go rounds with that job. Even in 2007, people in Delaware County were always prepared to see someone like me when I had to do inspections. I was not prepared for how political that job was going to be. It was new to them, the residents where I worked, seeing an African American coming from my neighborhood.

Sometimes I had to go way out in the county. I had never seen rural areas like that. I told John, "Hey, this ain't like the inner city, man. When I was young, I would maybe see a stray raccoon in the garbage can at Parkview Apartments. But I mean, when you're out there in the country, you see deer. You see foxes. Not quite like the projects."

One day I was out in the county to inspect a modular home, and it was going to be a long, hot day. Modular homes had to be checked for safety in the electrical systems and in the foundations. I focused especially on the footers underneath the homes which were made of cinder block and rebar. The footers kept the home grounded and safe. I made sure each one was deep enough, and checked the frost line, to make sure it could handle all kinds of weather. Usually people knew I was helping them and didn't mind seeing me coming.

As a building commissioner, I always tried to dress professionally. But I was digging around under houses and was going to get dirty, so I wore boots and jeans for that. Because I dressed casually, at first, someone might not understand what I was doing there.

I had been there a while when I saw an older gentleman, maybe 80 years old, driving out on a golf cart with this hound dog. I immediately got the impression that they didn't like seeing me there. The dog was growling and barking. I smiled and waved. The man gave no reaction at first, and then said, "Hey, boy!"

Now let me explain here a minute. I don't care where you live, but you should know you don't call a black guy a "boy." But I said to myself, "Ok, I'm not going to worry about that. He is an older, white man. He might have been raised that way." But I was uncomfortable knowing I was probably the only African American for miles around.

I realized I've got my shirt off, so I took my ID out to show him and introduced myself. I said, "How are you doing, sir?"

Then he said, "It's a surprise to see you niggers out here in this neck of the woods."

I swallowed a minute. I was thinking like, "Man, am I seeing and hearing things? This is the 2000s. What in the world is going on out here? Like, whoa!"

Then, I said, "I'm just here to check the footer, sir. How are you doing?" Then I heard a car gunning up the drive. This time it was a young white man. Maybe this was his grandfather. He was younger, but he wasn't any better. They both started talking like that to me. "Nigger this, and nigger that."

But I had to get this job done. And it was going to take several hours. So, I just went on working under that house in the heat. I even had to use their restroom. And the whole time they talked like that to me. Can you imagine?

When I was done, I just said, "You guys passed inspection. You guys can go ahead and cement up. You can go ahead and put the foundation up. Good luck. You're gonna have a beautiful modular home." I was always professional. Nobody in the world, nobody could break me.

As I was leaving, I could see that old guy chugging a beer, an old-style malt liquor. Now I didn't drink alcohol. I don't drink anything stronger than apple juice anymore because of my kidneys. But I sure could have used a cold ice water. Neither one of them offered.

As I was leaving, the older guy said, "Come here, boy."

I said, "No, sir. I got another inspection I got to deal with."

He said, "You know, you're different from some of those niggers."

I said, "Thank you, sir! I think different about you, too. Have a good day."

It was all I could do to walk confidently to my car. When I got far enough away, I was shaking. I got very, very angry. When I got in the car, I was so angry I started crying. I could not believe this was modern day. I sat and watched those guys for a minute. They were going around closing the door like nothing was wrong, like nothing bad or unusual just happened.

I was thinking, "There are two ways I could handle this. Now, Marwin, you know how you would have reacted in your old life? I could take that truck, a four-by-four, and run them over. Or, I could just leave." I wasn't that person anymore. I had to be the example now, even to them. I treated people better than that, and I had a family to feed.

So, I just backed up, peeled off and went back to the office. The worst thing was, at that time, I had inherited some problems as building inspector. Sadly, my secretary at the time acted very prejudiced, too. I was still working on that situation which was resolved later. But that day, I walked in and said to her, "Hello there. I'm back from the county, but I am about to go on home." She said, "What's wrong, Marwin? Where are you going, boy? You going home already today? You being lazy?" I said, "Nah. I'm just not feeling well. That is going to do it for today." Yes, I was her boss, and she talked that way to me.

When I got home that night, I wondered if I could go back to that job the next day. I thought of giving up. I said to myself, "I can't deal with this stuff no more." But I had just gotten my first home. I said to myself, "Man, I've got a mortgage to pay. I can't quit this job. And, I have got to be an example to my children. I have a job to do."

By the next morning, I put on my suit and tie. I was ready. When I got to the office, I saw a letter laying on my desk. It was from John Brooke and the other county commissioners. It said, "Marwin, we really appreciate how you were being such a professional on your inspection in the county yesterday. We got a phone call from some neighbors there who said you were being called racist names, but you still were such a professional."

I said to myself, "See Marwin, you always had it. You can always figure out how to deal with these challenges in life." The way I saw it, people just really didn't understand, especially if they were older. Some people forgot the reason for the word nigger. This word was used by slave masters. It described a slave as a lowdown dirty person. The slave masters used it to try to belittle people, to make them feel like they were "less than." Some people say even now, "Oh, being a slave. That was so long ago. You just got to forget about it." But with people still around behaving like that?

I had to move forward, but I did not have to forget.

As part of the Ball State University welcoming team, Marwin greeted former President Barack Obama during his first campaign run (2007).

CHAPTER 16

ANOINTED WITH RESPONSIBILITIES

"Now the name Marwin Strong was out there not as the drug dealer— my name meant something different"

In retrospect, I was glad I hung on in that position as the building commissioner. It was an honor, and I believe God chose me to take it on. He did not promise it would be easy. In fact, I know He told me it would be hard. I was charged to make sure people were safe in their homes. I was treated well by most people.

The harder I worked, the more responsibility and accolades I received. The City of Muncie appointed me to the city's hiring board. That was an honor. We were responsible for hirings in all departments of the city. It wasn't done by the mayor as you might think.

Then, I was also blessed to be appointed as a member of the first city/county Human Rights Commission Board. At one time, the board appointed me as president. I'm like, "Whoa, this is cool!" I got to help hire the first Director of the Human Rights Commission, Yvonne Thompson. She was the first! I was so proud that I got to be one of the ones who hired her. As of this writing, she is still there doing great things.

The Human Rights Commission made sure people got a chance to be treated equally and fairly. It was ground-breaking at the time and necessary. People of different colors, genders and orientations could not be sure they were getting a fair shake without it.

Anybody could file a civil complaint about discrimination. That included everything from housing discrimination, job discrimination, sexual orientation and gender discrimination. For example, someone who could not get approved by a landlord to be a renter, but who had good credit, they could sue for housing discrimination if they thought they were being treated differently based on one of the protected categories. Let's say today, you had someone of different sexual orientation. Indiana still has laws on the books banning marriage with same sex couples even though the Supreme Court passed the federal law (Indiana Lawyer, 2020). So, let's say this person says, "Hey, I have seen four or five other people, who have partners of a different gender, and they got approved in this neighborhood, but the same managers will not approve my application because they don't like that I'm gay."

The Commission had a lot of power to research and decide these cases. Once the commission had a complaint, it could assign an independent party to investigate. Based on the research, the parties could get mediation or even go to court. The commission had subpoena power to call a potential offender to court. We had a direct link to the EEOC (Equal Employment Opportunity Commission) at the State office in Indianapolis. Sometimes the state would even research the case. Getting away with discrimination was going to be a lot harder with the commission in place. I knew I was not the only one who had experienced discrimination. I was able to do something about it.

My leadership in the county, and with the Enough is Enough movement, gave me one of the biggest honors of my life. I won the chance to meet presidential candidate Barack Obama when he came to Ball State in 2007. I was one of his greeters. I got to meet the future President of the United States; the first President who was a black man. Now, that's something. We were even wearing the same suit and tie combo!

The more responsibility I had, the more I wanted to do. Then, God opened the door to do just that. I met my friend Allison Bell for the first time in 2004. At the time, she was the first managing director of a special project called Partners for Community Impact. Partners was a community development initiative funded by the United Way of Delaware County, the Lilly Endowment Inc., Ball Memorial Hospital (BMH) Foundation, Inc., the Ball Brothers Foundation, the George and Frances Ball Foundation and the Muncie and Delaware County Community Foundation.

Allison explained that Partners was bringing people and groups together around top community issues and getting funds for projects to help solve them. One initiative very close to my heart was the Weed & Seed program. Weed and Seed was going to help people I cared about. I still worried about my homies getting out of drugs, off the streets and into jobs.

Partners was going for a million dollar grant from the U.S. Department of Justice. Weed & Seed grants helped communities cut crime by improving neighborhood policing to "weed" it out. It also provided plans for coordinated prisoner reentry services for those leaving prison. We helped to "seed" anti-crime efforts by helping them get basic needs met including jobs. That's what would keep them from committing crimes and ending up in jail again.

It was a massive group effort. We got everybody involved from government, social service agencies, churches and law enforcement. We had the mayor, the police chief and sheriff departments and prosecutors involved. But all these groups served on both sides to give perspectives on both the weeding, law enforcement efforts, and the seeding side.

Partners asked me to be a co-chair of the Seed side. This was a perfect fit with Enough is Enough. We had to formulate a five-year plan to put these in place. This plan had to be supported by research with statistics, maps, proof of resources and personnel to prove we deserved the grant. It took months of work, but we did it.

We were focusing on housing, food and jobs, including for those who had been convicted of felonies. There were large numbers coming back to downtown Muncie every year (MWS, 2008).

Yes, it was discouraging. But we kept looking for new angles. If we wanted to reduce people's dependence on drugs and violence, we had to find ways for them to make honest money. Many of those I talked with said, "Marwin, what are you gonna give me? I tried getting a steady job, but nothing come of it." I wanted to offer them some hope. I understood. If these people couldn't make money with drugs, they can't just let their families starve.

It was especially hard for people coming out of prison. Former inmates would say to me, "Hey, Marwin. I went out there to get a job. I went to the employment office, and I worked 60 days in the trial period. But then they let me go. I cannot get full-time employment because I've had a felony. I got to go back out there and sell drugs. I understand what you're saying, Marwin, that I need to give up this life. But I got to sell drugs, man. I got to feed my family!"

We reached out to businesses and asked them if they would hire felons in some cases. Our group took responsibility for mentoring these future employees. We said, "Hey, this person needs a job. Would you be willing to hire someone with a felony?" We explained to businesses that there were benefits they could get by hiring felons, including tax exemptions. Our group mentored people coming out of prison. We made sure the workers didn't have a bad drug test.

This group also developed lists of employers who would hire felons. We called it the Friendly Felony job list. It is still at the Delaware County Community Corrections office. We distributed the list to the local jails, police officers, sheriff's deputies and other local non-profits. We also developed lists of social services that helped people coming out of incarceration. Many agencies offered relief on utility bills, shelter and food, but not all accepted felons for their programs. That was part of the problem for people who had been in jail.

The project lasted several years. Once we got the Weed & Seed grant, although she did not want to leave the effort, Allison had to move on to another job for personal reasons. In late 2008, Greg Maynard joined the group as managing director of Partners for Community Impact. Along with Greg, and all the others in the group, we got to implement the Seed programs.

We even won national recognition for one of our Seed projects. We planned a basketball tournament to bring youth and law enforcement together. Young people from poverty-stricken neighborhoods would play on teams, and law enforcement officers would be coaches, referees or organizers. It was so successful we got recognized as an example for other Weed & Seed communities all over the country.

People in downtown Muncie had special opportunities to come together to understand each other, and crime rates started to go down. In fact, crime went down each year from 2004 to 2007 (MWS, 2008).

In addition, a later study of community member surveys showed that, for the most part, residents had positive impressions of law enforcement. That was true for all groups except African Americans. So, we still had a lot to do. We will always need to work for improvements. But I was grateful to be a part of the success we had. I know we helped make a difference (McCann, 2019).

Accomplishing progress in our community filled me with genuine satisfaction and pride in my community. I thought about myself and how far I had come.

Now the name Marwin Strong was out there not as the drug dealer. My name meant something different.

I was not drinking. I was not smoking. I did not have to watch my back like in my drug days. I was vibrant and energetic. This was the life God promised me. I started a brand, new life…a brand, new life.

Marwin with his Ball Memorial Hospital angel, Nurse Jan Carter-Goldman, reunited at a Muncie Out-of-Towner's Reunion, "Back to Muncie Fest" (2019).

CHAPTER 17

MY CUP RUNNETH OVER

"So, I did what someone else did for me—
I paid it forward"

Just because you are saved doesn't mean life never gets hard again. God did not promise me that the good times would last forever. In 2010, I lost my job as building commissioner because of politics. John Brooke and some other commissioners moved on, and the new commissioners ordered the county offices to cut their budgets. My county building commissioner office was consolidated with another city office. So, people in my office were on the chopping block, including me.

I still had a lot of work to do to improve lives in Muncie. It just was going to be somewhere new and different. I wasn't going to let job setbacks stop me. I was working for the kids in my neighborhoods in my hometown, and I was not going to quit. I tried to make sure nobody knew the pain of that situation for me. I turned to friends in the community who were there for me. It proved again how much mentorship means in success in life.

Just as God promised, He was there for me. I got another chance of a lifetime to go in a new direction and start my teaching career. I was asked to be a speaker for a class at Ball State University by a good friend, Nancy Harper. After my visit, we discussed teaching the class together. It was for NCAA players to help them keep up their grades, and to start career planning, while playing sports in college. For five years, Nancy and I taught a class together. I then taught at Ivy Tech as a life and study skills instructor. It was about college prep and career planning. Especially at the community college, I knew I was helping students who were living in poverty and violence like I had.

After teaching in college, the K through 12 district, Muncie Community Schools, hired me to teach in the

Jobs for America Graduates, or JAG program. This was for at-risk students who needed credit recovery. I helped them with classes and to focus on employment, workforce readiness and getting a job while they were in school. I also got to go back to one of my first loves, basketball. I got to coach the school basketball team! As part of that basketball program, I worked hard to be a role model in the classroom and on the court.

The hard part of working in inner-city schools was that, once again, I was seeing first-hand how many kids were getting lost to drugs and violence. It was so discouraging. I knew where some of my students were headed. I tried to stop it.

I warned them, "You gotta quit what you're doin'. I'm in tune with the police department. Go talk to your young brother, man, talk to your friends. If they don't stop doin' what they're doin', we're gonna get 'em." They trusted me.

Most of the students were struggling with poverty just like I did. You know how many times I saw kids running around with holey shoes? That reminded me of my slip and slides when I first tried out for the basketball team years ago. So, I did what someone else did for me. I paid it forward.

Every season, I would get new shoes for all the team members. The first time it happened was great. I asked each of them, "What size shoe do you wear?" They each told me. Next thing they knew, they had a nice pair of Michael Jordan's in their lockers. They were like, "Wow! Where did these come from?"

Parents said to me, "Hey, Mr. Strong, I had a light bill due, 134 dollars. Here you are paying for my kid's shoes. You know how much I appreciate you doing that? Thank you for buying him some tennis shoes. I could go ahead and pay my light bill because it was you that bought him new tennis shoes."

You know why I got basketball shoes for my teams I coached every year? I did it because a guy named Coach Lafferty did that for me. Coach Lafferty was a father figure to me through it all. He had seen something in me I hadn't seen myself. He had been there throughout my life. Now, you think about it. We got two different races. I'm African American. He's white. It showed me, even in a low-income black neighborhood where I came from, that heart has no color.

I could always call him about anything. The money he blessed me with throughout my life was incredible. I can't even tell you how much he spent on me. Coach

Lafferty was my mentor. He was my friend for life. He was there for me, and believed in me, even when I had hard times as an adult. I miss him to this day. He died in 2014. I cried that day. I did. So, getting shoes for my basketball players was my way of paying it forward. It was my way to return the good that God had given me.

During a game time-out, Marwin coached his Texas Can Oak-Cliff Cougars Basketball Team (2019).

Marwin Strong for Muncie City Council at-Large campaign poster (2017).

CHAPTER 18

BECOMING A SHEPHERD

"I didn't want to be labeled as a race;
I wanted people to judge me on my character"

I found out late in life that my family members weren't all black sheep. I had leadership experience in my blood. I found out my uncle, Albert Johnson, was the first African American city council member at-large in the City of Muncie years ago. So, in 2011, I decided to run for city council at-large to serve the people of Muncie like my uncle did.

I was surprised that a lot of people I knew tried to discourage me from running. I would tell people, "I'm running for city council at-large as a Democrat. I'm from the community and live and work here. I know the community and want to help." Some family and friends would say, "What are you putting yourself out like that for? You ain't gonna win." Some people even told me, "We're gonna make sure you don't win." I guess they were honest.

But I did have lots of supporters. Many people in the community came to meetings, raised money and even rallied in the streets with me. But the ugly head of racism, even another eight years later, was still there.

On voting day, candidates could put campaign signs at polling centers. These were official voting centers by law, so I didn't expect to have problems. At six o'clock in the morning, I went to the Ross Center, a polling place in one of the historically white areas. This was one of the areas where I really couldn't go when I was a kid because it was dangerous for me. But it was 2011, right?

So, I'm putting my sign in the yard of the polling place, and two big guys approached me. They said, "Hey Nigger, why you putting this poll sign out here?" At that time, nobody was out there yet but me and these two white guys. So, I didn't want to start a fight. I just put my sign in the front of the building as I was supposed to and left. About an hour later, after I had finished putting up other signs at other voting locations, I came back to check on that sign. When I got there, that poll sign was nowhere around.

I thought, "Well, at least that guy was honest. He told me I would not get any votes there. He just told me flat out. There's no need to put your sign out here." I guess I could have saved the money.

That wasn't the only place I had a sign stolen. Another time, I had a big expensive banner against drugs and violence that I put up in my old neighborhood. I had used it many times in public places and no one ever bothered it. This time it was down on Madison Street near the McDonald's where I used to hang out for meals. It was stolen. I had raised 800 dollars to make that sign, with pictures of my kids on it, about reducing drugs and violence. Somebody stole it, just ripped it off.

I didn't win that race for city council. It was a hard blow to me. I did think to myself, "Why am I staying in Muncie? Maybe I should pick up and move somewhere else." I didn't want to do that. Muncie was my city.

I prayed about it every day. I asked God, "What do you want me to do?" I wanted to serve my community. I even thought of running for mayor one day. I was so embedded and invested in Muncie. You know how football players put shoulder pads on? It's like I got shoulder pads and Muncie was my shoulder pads. I've carried them around wherever I went. If I leave, then who's going to carry those shoulder pads? Who is going to rally in the streets to end the drugs and violence? Who is going to have the basketball tournaments that bring youth and law enforcement together?

I wanted to be the first African American to be mayor of this city. I wanted to serve everybody in any party, Democrats, Independents and Republicans. But you had gaps. Racism was still there. Some people didn't want to see me succeed. Some people didn't want any African American to succeed. You had people who are racist, and you had people who just don't want change. I even got push back from some African Americans.

It was hard being a black male in the spotlight. Some people I grew up with couldn't see me for anything except what I was. I guess part of it could have been jealousy. Some people only want you to go to a certain level. Because of our culture on both sides, in some people's eyes I'm still a nigger. If I'm succeeding, then someone else is not. That troubles me. Why is it either or, and not that both succeed?

Dr. Martin Luther King, Jr. explained, I don't want to be labeled as a race; I want people to judge me on my character. Judge me on my integrity. Judge me on my actions. Don't judge me on my color (King, 1964). I'm not even all African American. I'm Cherokee, Indian, too. No one is all the way African American or all white. Most of us are not just one race. How can we deny part of ourselves in others?

When I ran for city council member at-large in 2011, I said I wanted to go into the race as a servant, not as a politician. When it come sto "real politicians" in the United States of America, that word politician leaves a bad taste in your mouth.

A servant leader is different. It's not just about knocking door-to-door. It's not just about shaking hands. A servant politician gets down and does the work for the people. I was working for the people of Muncie, not in spite of other people.

For example, when you go to the finest restaurant the servers come and say, "What would you like to drink?" You might say water. Then they give you a couple of minutes and come back. They give you time to see what you really want to drink and eat. They're serving you. They want to find out what you need. And they don't leave in the middle of your meal. They come back and check on you. They'll help you out if there's a problem with your food.

That's what I wanted to be in the community of Muncie. I didn't want to be named as a "politician." I wanted to be a servant. No matter what race, what creed or what gender you were, no matter where you came from, no matter what background you had, I'd

Marwin preached a sermon, based on the Book of James, entitled "I Got to Get Myself Together" at True Vine Holiness Tabernacle in Muncie, Indiana (2020).

still be serving you, myself, in that office. I just had to find how I could be a shepherd some other way.

Speaking at New Life Holy Tabernacle in Indianapolis, Indiana (2016).

Marwin at Texas Can Oak-Cliff Academy in Dallas, Texas (2019).

CHAPTER 19

FOLLOW ME ALL THE DAYS OF MY LIFE

"It's not about me"

I loved my Muncie community, and I never intended to leave. I had continued success in the Enough is Enough movement and in my jobs at Muncie Community Schools. Once again, God had other plans. Muncie Community Schools lost funds because of the population dropping. The city had to consolidate schools and drop teacher positions. Once again, I got laid off.

I needed a job that paid well, and I was running out of work options in Muncie. I had high hopes for a political career. But I had kids to send to school. Running for office would cost money. And until I won an election, there wouldn't be enough money to live on. I had to be open to moving on somewhere else and starting over.

I asked God, "Where do I go to continue my journey and service?" He told me, "Sometimes we must go where we are needed."

But I worried about leaving Muncie. What would happen to the Enough is Enough movement? Would there be even more killings again? Of course, many amazing people, Muncie organizations, government offices and churches were fighting against drugs and violence every day. But losing an advocate can be hard, especially for a smaller community. There's always more work and fewer people to carry the load.

I also didn't want to leave my family. My momma and daddy were getting older. My momma wasn't well. God spoke to me through my momma. She sat me down next to her and said, "Marwin you are always doing everything for everybody else. What is Marwin gonna do for Marwin?"

I just stopped. I hadn't thought about that for years. That's what was missing. What did I want to do? Sometimes finding your next assignment from God is about looking inside yourself. I didn't have to deny myself to serve. If I'm true to God, my mission and my way of life, I could serve anywhere. I loved travel. I loved sharing my mission. I was excited to see what else was out there for me.

I looked up a job on the website Indeed.com focusing on my mission and what I wanted to do. The most intriguing job was for a teacher at an academy for at-risk youth. It was in Dallas, Texas. I thought, "Well, here goes. Let go and let God!"

Can you believe this? The leaders of this academy called me that week. They said, "Marwin, we don't know what it is about you. But you jump off the page of this resume. We can't believe what you've accomplished in your life. We want you to come interview with us."

I was so shocked. Dallas, Texas? Yup. The Big City.

So, the Texas Can Academy flew me down there. It was beautiful and the school's leadership, programs and successes were amazing. The school had middle and high school prep classes including AP classes for advanced courses that give college credit. We talked about salary and opportunities to do other jobs within the school. I was impressed.

I said to myself, "I could be a part of this. It's anti-drugs and violence. It's resources for getting out of poverty. It's helping youth stay out of trouble and have new opportunities." So, I told them, "Sold!"

You should have seen my truck. I drove cross country with all my belongings nearly 1,000 miles. I could hear God saying, "Everything is gonna be alright, Marwin. New is good. Go on Southwest, young man. Keep going Southwest."

I've been at Texas Can Academy for two years now. I teach AP English, persuasive writing, life skills and career planning. I'm seeing success! Many of my Dallas students have moved on from rough backgrounds to full-time jobs. Some go off to college.

I go into class every day with a suit and tie because I'm an example. When I start with a new class, I always ask them what kind of background they think I come from. They'll say, "Mr. Strong, you probably grew up in a nice house. Your momma or daddy was probably a doctor or something." Then, I tell them the truth.

I can still mix it up with Ebonics. I speak two languages so I can speak to youth in a way that makes sense to them. It's still a part of me, too. I tell the kids about the poverty, the crime, the drugs and the violence I experienced as a child. They're astounded to hear what I went through.

Most of these kids know about living with a lack of food, a lack of adults around and a lack of hope. Many of them are still there. I'm there to help and show progress is possible despite discouragement, despite job loss, despite illness and despite depression. I give them tools to help like critical thinking, problem solving, research and life-long learning. I help prepare them to be economically independent. I tell them, "You know, man. I have done it. You can too. That's what it's about."

What about basketball? I got that reward, too. I'm now the head basketball coach for the school team. This team hadn't had a winning season in years. We didn't win it all last year, but we ended up going to the championships. And of course, I gave all the kids on this team new shoes as well, of course. I've got to write a whole different book to tell you about that.

You ready for the biggest twist of all? I found my way to the NBA. Dallas, Texas is home to the NBA team, the Mavericks. I met the owner Mark Cuban who told me about their youth summer basketball camps every year. These are ones like I used to go to. So now I'm coaching every summer with the Mavericks. It's awesome, man!

Thanks to God, my table is full. I'm teaching classes, coaching the school team and coaching for the NBA in the summer. I'm also speaking around the country about strategies to reduce drugs and violence.

God brought me back from death's door. I could still be dealing drugs or in jail. I could be dead. But He brought me back to work for others. I love my new life. I miss Muncie and my family. But I go back and forth to visit. My concept of home has just gotten bigger.

Anything I do in life is because I want to be an example of hope. This is from the heart. God brought me back from the shadow of death into the light. I escaped the fire. I chose to follow Him on the right path. Staying in line with your own goals and mission for success isn't a ball and chain. It's freedom.

I have the freedom to choose to answer my calling. And there ain't nothing gonna stop me from answerin' it.

On a visit from Dallas, Marwin visited with family on the porch of his Muncie home (2018).

Marwin on a community activism speaking engagement in Atlanta, Georgia (2017).

BIBLIOGRAPHY

2 Corinthians 5:18-20 ESV — All this is from God, who through — Bible Gateway. (2001). *Bible Gateway.* Crossway Bibles. https://www.biblegateway.com/passage/?search=2+Corinthians+5%3A18-20&version=ESV

Juvenile. (1998). 400 Degreez [Recorded by Juvenile]. Cash Money Records.

Aguiar, J. (2014, December 11). Charlie Titus — UMass Boston's longtime basketball coach — to leave bench behind, remain on staff. Dorchester Reporter; *Boston Neighborhood News,* Inc. https://www.dotnews.com/2014/charlie-titus-umass-boston-s-longtime-basketball-coach-leave-bench-beh

Ahmad, F., Rossen, L., & Sutton, P. (2020). Products — Vital Statistics Rapid Release — Provisional Drug Overdose Data. Center for Disease Control and Prevention. https://www.cdc.gov/nchs/nvss/vsrr/drug-overdose-data.htm

Assistant Coaches. (1997). MIT — Massachusetts Institute of Technology. http://web.mit.edu/landerso/bb_www2/Assistant_Coaches.html

Bond, J. M., & Herman, MD. PhD., A. A. (2016, July). Lagging Life Expectancy for Black Men: A Public Health Imperative. PubMed Central (PMC); U.S. National Libraries of Medicine, National Institutes of Health. https://www.ncbi.nlm.nih.gov/pmc/articles/PMC4984780/

de la Bastide, K. (2017, Nov. 9). Tragedy Transformed Ten Point Coalition Founder's Life's Direction. Local News. Heraldbulletin.com. *The Herald Bulletin.*
https://www.heraldbulletin.com/news/local_news/tragedy-transformed-ten-point-coalition-founders-lifes-direction/article_a89ec7d4-9997-55dd-9d4b-f3b9668d14b3.html

Church, N. (2016, January 18). *What does the Bible say about racism?* Newspring Church.
https://newspring.cc/articles/is-racism-a-sin

Clipping from *The Star Press;* Bing Crosby Obituary — Newspapers.com. (2010, April 29). Newspapers.com by Ancestry.
https://www.newspapers.com/clip/9851216/the-star-press/

Demographic Differences in Sentencing. United States Sentencing Commission. (2017, November 14). United States Sentencing Commission.
https://www.ussc.gov/research/research-reports-demographic-differences-sentencing

Diaz, M. C. (2015, October 16). *"Faith is taking the first step even when you don't see the whole staircase".* Camistok.Wordpress.com.
https://camistok.wordpress.com/2015/10/16/the-meaning-of-faith-by-martin-luther-king/

Drug overdose death rates are higher in rural areas than urban areas. (2017, October 19). CDC Newsroom. U.S. Department of Health & Human Services.
https://www.cdc.gov/media/releases/2017/p1019-rural-overdose-deaths.html

Ephesians 2:14-18 ESV — For he himself is our peace, who has — (2001). Bible Gateway. Crossway Bibles.
https://www.biblegateway.com/passage/?search=Ephesians+2%3A14-18&version=ESV

Fitchburg State College vs UMass Boston Beacons (11/28/03 at Boston, MA — Clark Athletic Center) — UMass Boston Athletics. (2003, November 28). UMass Boston Athletics. University of Massachusetts Boston.
https://www.beaconsathletics.com/sports/m-baskbl/2003-04/files/game1.htm

FY 2008 Weed and Seed Communities Application, Muncie Weed & Seed, Southern District of Indiana. (2008). Muncie Action Plan, Weed & Seed Steering Committee.
http://muncieactionplan.net/wp-content/uploads/2016/10/Muncie-WS-Final-with-Maps.pdf

Guzik, D. (2011). *Study Guide for Psalm 23 by David Guzik.* Blue Letter Bible.
http://www.blueletterbible.org/Comm/guzik_david/StudyGuide_Psa/Psa_23.cfm

Hebrews 13:3 ESV — Remember those who are in prison, as — Bible Gateway. (n.d.). *Bible Gateway.* Retrieved May 28, 2020, from https://www.biblegateway.com/passage/?search=Hebrews+13%3A3&version=ESV

Herrick, G. (2011). *An Exposition of Psalm 23. Bible.Org Where the World Comes to Study the Bible.* Blue Letter Bible.
https://bible.org/article/exposition-psalm-23

Hutson, MD, H. R., Anglin, MD, D., & Eckstein, MD, M. (1996, April). *Drive-by Shootings by Violent Street Gangs in Los Angeles: A Five-year Review from 1989 to 1993.* Wiley Online Library. John Wiley & Sons, Inc.
https://onlinelibrary.wiley.com/doi/abs/10.1111/j.1553-2712.1996.tb03441.x

James 1:19-20 ESV — Hearing and Doing the Word — Know this, — Bible Gateway. (n.d.). Bible Gateway. Retrieved May 28, 2020, from

https://www.biblegateway.com/
passage/?search=James+1%3A19-20&version=ESV

John 16:33 ESV — I have said these things to you, that — Bible Gateway. (n.d.). Bible Gateway. Retrieved May 28, 2020, from https://www.biblegateway.com/
passage/?search=John+16%3A33&version=ESV

Justice, National Center for Juvenile & Delinquency Prevention. (2017, Oct. 25). *State Residential Placement Rates by Race/Ethnicity, 2017. Home Office of Juvenile Justice and Delinquency Prevention.* Office of Juvenile Justice and Delinquency Prevention. https://www.ojjdp.gov/ojstatbb/corrections/qa08203.asp?qaDate=2017

Kellogg, N. C. (2018, May 28). *Top Effects of Poverty. The Borgen Project.* The Borgen Project.
https://borgenproject.org/5-effects-poverty/

King, Jr., M. L. (1964, August 28). *I Have a Dream. The Nobel Prize.* Nobel Media AB.
https://www.nobelprize.org/prizes/peace/1964/
king/26141-i-have-a-dream/

King, Jr., M. L. (1967, reprinted March 7, 2018). *Martin Luther King Jr. Speech: 'The Three Evils' of Society* — The Atlantic Monthly Group.
https://www.theatlantic.com/magazine/archive/2018/02/
martin-luther-king-hungry-club-forum/552533/

Matthews, R. A. (2018, January 15). *Opinion: Martin Luther King Jr. knew the answer to racism.* The Mercury News.
https://www.mercurynews.com/2018/01/15/
opinion-martin-luther-king-jr-knew-the-answer/amp/

McCann, A., Minsky-Kelly, D., & Stewart, K. (2019, December 16). *Most Caring Cities in America*. WalletHub; Evolution Finance, Inc.
https://wallethub.com/edu/most-caring-cities/17814/

MIT Men's Basketball 1997-'98 Summary: Season in Review. (1998). MIT — Massachusetts Institute of Technology.
http://web.mit.edu/bball/www/1998/summary.html

Muncie, Indiana (IN) profile: population, maps, real estate, averages, homes, statistics, relocation, travel, jobs, hospitals, schools, crime, moving, houses, news, sex offenders. (n.d.). City-Data.Com - Stats about All US Cities - Real Estate, Relocation Info, Crime, House Prices, Cost of Living, Races, Home Value Estimator, Recent Sales, Income, Photos, Schools, Maps, Weather, Neighborhoods, and More. City-Data.com. Retrieved May 28, 2020, from
https://www.city-data.com/city/Muncie-Indiana.html

Munroe, Charity. *Tales Told Out of School: Ball State University African American Oral History Project II. Cardinal Scholar*. Ball State University, Aug. 2018,
http://147.226.7.105/bitstream/handle/123456789/201648/2018MunroCharity-combined.pdf?sequence=1&isAllowed=y

NBA History. (2020, May 28). NBAHOOPSONLINE.Com: NBA Hoops Online.
https://nbahoopsonline.com/History/

Newman, K. (2019, October 9). *Retirement of Vice Chancellor Charlie Titus*. University of Massachusetts Boston.
https://www.umb.edu/the_university/chancellor/communications/retirement_of_vice_chancellor_charlie_titus

Papadinis, T. (2017). *The Paula Titus Scholarship Fund*. UMass Boston Alumni.
http://www.alumni.umb.edu/s/1355/campaign/index.aspx?sid=1355&gid=3&pgid=6866

Revelation 7:9-10 ESV — A Great Multitude from Every Nation —
  Bible Gateway. (2001). Bible Gateway. Crossway Bibles.
  https://www.biblegateway.com/
  passage/?search=Revelation+7%3A9-10&version=ESV

Sabol, W. J. (2019, December). *Trends in Correctional Control by Race*
  and Sex. Prison Policy Initiative. Council on Criminal Justice,
  Washington.
  https://cdn.ymaws.com/counciloncj.org/resource/
  collection/4683B90A-08CF-493F-89ED-A0D7C4BF7551/
  Trends_in_Correctional_Control_-_FINAL.pdf

Sauter, M. B. (2018, October 10). *Faces of poverty: What racial, social*
  groups are more likely to experience it? USA Today, a division of
  Gannett Satellite Information Network, LLC.
  https://www.usatoday.com/story/money/economy/2018/10/10/
  faces-poverty-social-racial-factors/37977173/

Scrap over old Indiana gay marriage ban derails popular bill - The
  Indiana Lawyer. (n.d.). The Indiana Lawyer; Associated Press.
  Retrieved May 28, 2020, from
  https://www.theindianalawyer.com/articles/
  scrap-over-old-indiana-gay-marriage-ban-derails-popular-bill

Smith Pegues, D. (2020, May 27). *6 Ways to Resist Racism - TD Jakes.*
  T. D. Jakes Enterprises.
  https://www.tdjakes.com/posts/6-ways-to-resist-racism?fb_
  comment_id=1406171759407824_15775131056070
  21

Smith, S. (2020, May 27). *What Does the Bible Say About Education?*
  Crossway Bibles.
  https://www.openbible.info/topics/education

Sulanke, K. (2020, May 28). *11 Delaware County Non-Profits Receive $200k in Grant Funding*. Muncie Journal. Woof Boom Radio.

http://www.munciejournal.com/2020/01/alliance-magazine-muncies-robust-philanthropic-profile-leads-indianas-major-cities

Theoharis, J. (2020, January 17). *Martin Luther King and the 'polite' racism of white liberals — The Washington Post*. Washington Post. https://www.washingtonpost.com/nation/2020/01/17/martin-luther-king-polite-racism-white-liberals/?outputType=amp

Vallas, R., & Boteach, M. (2014, September 17). *The Top 10 Solutions to Cut Poverty and Grow the Middle Class - Center for American Progress*. Center for American Progress. https://www.americanprogress.org/ issues/poverty/news/2014/09/17/97287/ the-top-10-solutions-to-cut-poverty-and-grow-the-middle-class/

Walls, E. (2017, April 1). *Psalm 23 — First Presbyterian Church: Alexandria, PA*. First Presbyterian Church: Alexandria, PA. https://apchurch.org/2017/04/01/2026/

What does the Bible say about racism? (2016, January 18). NewSpring. Cc. Newspring Church. https://newspring.cc/articles/is-racism-a-sin

ABOUT THE AUTHOR

Elder Marwin Strong is currently an Advanced Placement English teacher and basketball coach at Dallas Texas Can Academy Charter-Oak Cliff School, a program that offers a second chance to stu-  dents who have struggled in a traditional high school setting. Prior to moving to Dallas, Strong was a long-time community leader in Muncie and was ordained as an elder at New Life Ministries in Indianapolis. Strong is also a leader at The Potter's House, a non-denominational American megachurch in Dallas, Texas. The church is led by well-known pastor, author and filmmaker T.D. Jakes. Jakes's church services and evangelistic sermons are broadcast as The Potter's Touch.

While Strong is committed to sharing his mission in Texas, he continues to support his mission in Muncie. He supervises his Enough is Enough movement continuing with outreach to people returning to the community from prison.

With a bachelor's from Ball State University and an associate degree from Ivy Tech Community College in Legal Studies, Strong is a consultant conducting lectures and training on theories of classroom engagement with an emphasis on multiculturalism. He speaks at colleges, community organizations and churches across the United States and overseas. Strong is committed to providing opportunities for better education, better economic opportunities and multicultural understanding across the globe.

ABOUT THE EDITOR

Allison (A. K.) Bell is a writer and editor in Muncie, Indiana. Bell started her career in journalism, reporting for local radio and television news stations in three states. She has also worked extensively in community advocacy and education while raising her children.

Bell met Marwin Strong in 2004 when she was managing director of Partners for Community Impact. In that position, she supervised grant applications and the development of social improvement projects including Weed & Seed.

In education, Bell developed curriculum, and produced live online and recorded classes for elementary, middle, high school and college students. Many of these programs were distributed nationally and internationally.

Bell has a Masters in Broadcast Journalism from Northwestern University and a Bachelor of Arts, in political science and French, from Duke University. She lives with her husband, Cesar Genders, and their many giant dogs, in Muncie, Indiana. They have five children, several honorary children and an increasing number of grandchildren. Bell's editing work on this book is dedicated to the memory of her parents Steve and Joyce Bell.

COMING NEXT

Marwin Strong and A. K. Bell are developing curriculum and resources for teachers about classroom engagement for at-risk youth. This will include strategies for in person and online classes.